CARDINAL XIMÉNEZ DE CISNEROS

Political Theory and Law
IN MEDIEVAL SPAIN

MARIE R. MADDEN, Ph.D.

Professor of Spanish History and Political Theory, Fordham University

FOREWORD

by

MOORHOUSE I. X. MILLAR, S.J.

Chairman, Graduate Faculty of Political Philosophy

THE LAWBOOK EXCHANGE, LTD.
Clark, New Jersey

ISBN 978-1-58477-497-6

Lawbook Exchange edition 2005, 2019

The quality of this reprint is equivalent to the quality of the original work.

THE LAWBOOK EXCHANGE, LTD.
33 Terminal Avenue
Clark, New Jersey 07066-1321

Please see our website for a selection of our other publications and fine facsimile reprints of classic works of legal history:
www.lawbookexchange.com

Library of Congress Cataloging-in-Publication Data

Madden, Marie R. (Marie Regina), b. 1887.
Political theory and law in medieval Spain / Marie R. Maden ; foreward by Moorhouse I.X. Millar.
p. cm.
Originally published: New York : Fordham University Press, 1930.
Includes bibliographical references and index.
ISBN 1-58477-497-5 (cloth : alk. paper)
1. Public law--Spain--History--To 1500. 2. Law, Medieval. 3. Spain--Politics and government--To 1479. I. Title.

KKT202.M33 2005
342.46—dc22

Printed in the United States of America on acid-free paper

Political Theory and Law
IN MEDIEVAL SPAIN

MARIE R. MADDEN, PH.D.

Professor of Spanish History and Political Theory, Fordham University

FOREWORD

by

MOORHOUSE I. X. MILLAR, S.J.

Chairman, Graduate Faculty of Political Philosophy

NEW YORK
FORDHAM UNIVERSITY PRESS
1930

To My Parents

CONTENTS

CONTENTS

PART II

ADMINISTRATIVE MACHINERY

FOREWORD

"Nothing less than a convulsion that will shake the globe to its center can ever restore the European nations to that liberty by which they were once so much distinguished." In these words of Burke we seem to have a prophecy of what is slowly but surely taking place as a result of the convulsions of the World War. In every country the need is being recognized of subjecting the prevailing systems of government and of law to the earnest judgment of reason and to the test of historical experience. One of the most cheering consequences of this is the reaction throughout the English-speaking world to the baneful influence of continental European theories. As Holdsworth has noted in his recent book entitled "Some Lessons From Our Legal History," "There is danger that students who have specialized in these continental theories and who know little of the spirit of our historic system of law may mislead those who know less." How true this danger was may be readily judged in the light of the confusion that has been introduced into the study of law and government in this country as a result of the teaching in our universities of philosophies and of legal doctrines imported mainly from Germany. As Holdsworth observes further, the menace from such importations lies fundamentally in the continental theories as to sovereignty. As he says,

> *The theory of sovereignty, and the analysis of its effects upon law, have tended to separate morals from law, and to draw a hard and fast line between moral and legal rights. It is for this reason that the ethical ideals, which*

were at the base of medieval and seventeenth century legal and political reasoning, and appeared both in Burke's speeches and in Blackstone's "Commentaries," tend to be replaced by considerations of expediency; and that the dominant aim of politics tends to become merely the securing of the greatest material advantage for the strongest party in the state. Necessarily this change has reacted on methods of political reasoning. Both in the Middle Ages and in the seventeenth century, political theories were deduced logically from fixed postulates. But in modern times, when no such fixed postulates are recognized, they have tended to become merely a series of generalizations arrived at inductively, sometimes from the teachings of history, and often merely from considerations of expediency. But the conclusions of a science, which proceeds on these lines, are far more indefinite and far less authoritative than they were in the days when its conclusions were assumed to be logical deductions from great moral or religious principles. In fact, under the influence of the indeterminate and conflicting ideals of various groups of modern politicians, they tend to become merely a repertoire of arguments for the particular thesis which the writer happens to favor. It is clear that this absence of fixed principle puts a dangerous weapon into the hands of legal and political theorists. They can make a case for their theories; and they may easily make converts from those who have learning enough to understand, and not learning enough to criticize.

In lieu of "those fixed moral and religious standards which medieval men possessed" Holdsworth suggests "that the study of history, and especially legal history, can be made to do something towards supplying their place." But one of the features of the problem of law and government little adverted to when approached from the historical point of view is the peculiar paradox that whereas the law of Protestant English-speaking countries is decidedly Catholic in its original fundamental principles, the legal tradition of the Latin and Catholic countries is fundamentally pagan in its underlying philosophy and anti-Christian in many of its principles. Failure to recognize this distinction and account for the paradoxical contrast between the two great legal systems has been for a century or more the source of much confusion on the part of both Catholics and non-Catholics in their attempts to theorize about law and government in general as well as in their efforts to criticize historically their own respective systems. The reason for such failure is two-fold. On the one hand, there was the concerted prejudice of the dominant Protestant mentality with its bias against all things Catholic which led to the utter elimination of any reference to Catholic sources and the evasion of all facts which might tend to substantiate anything like indebtedness to Catholic thought or Catholic principles. On the other hand, there was the assumption still prevalent among lawyers and historians generally that the institutions and principles of the Common Law were peculiar to the people of England from the beginning, or in other words, that the continental peoples were somehow committed to undiluted Roman Law in its original pagan forms from the days of Constantine on.

Just as in England a substitute for a genuine historical account of the origins of our law was sought in the attempt to explain its superiority in favor of liberty on the basis of the genial instincts of our Anglo-Saxon ancestors, so on the continent there has been a persistent tendency to read history backwards, with the result that the legal and historical mind impregnated with the categories of the Roman Law tradition is quite incapable of recognizing, let alone appreciating, the controlling principles at work in the early formation of Western Christendom. Maitland was among the first to deal a shattering blow to that preposterous bit of nineteenth century romanticism now known as the Teutonic Myth, and quite recently Powicke in his remarkable "Life of Stephen Langton" has conclusively established the definite origin in Catholic theology of the underlying principles of Magna Charta. A. J. Carlyle in his "History of Medieval Political Theory" did much to revolutionize in English-speaking countries the notion that England was peculiar in her law and institutions. As Professor Rafael Altamira pointed out in 1915 in a chapter entitled "Magna Carta and Spanish Medieval Jurisprudence," included among the "Magna Carta Commemoration Essays," Spain was in many respects far in advance of England. "In Spain," he says,

> *and chiefly in Leon and Castile even the servile classes of earlier ages had attained a great improvement of condition in 1215, and the liberties which were gradually being won, chiefly benefited the people in general, not an oligarchy of nobles. Even in Aragon, where later times were to bring a retrograde movement in respect of some inferior classes, the advantages actually attained were more widely diffused than in England; and we find the position of the lower classes better protected by a legislation in which they were regarded as important factors.*

How far this statement is from being an exaggeration is now made clear for the English-reading public in the pages of the present book. Dr. Madden has made an important contribution not only to the history of Spain but to the history of our own Anglo-American legal and political institutions as well. None can fail to recognize the difficulty of the task she has so bravely undertaken, or can question the thoroughness of her achievement. Its importance will best be appreciated by those who are abreast of the more exceptional work being done in the field of legal history. But even the layman in such subjects will find ample ground for edification in a more thorough understanding of constitutional government from a careful study of Dr. Madden's splendid exposition of the earlier Spanish experiment.

MOORHOUSE I. X. MILLAR, S.J.

ACKNOWLEDGEMENT

THE preparation of this book has been considerably lightened by the assistance of many who kindly gave of their learning and time. In particular my greatest obligations are to the Reverend Moorhouse I. X. Millar, S.J., Chairman of the Faculty of Political Philosophy in Fordham University, under whose direction I began the study of political theory and without whose constant encouragement, criticism and learning so generously shared, I would not have been able to write this essay; and to the Reverend Demetrius B. Zema, S.J., Chairman of the Faculty of History, for helpful suggestions and access to books I could not otherwise have secured. I wish to acknowledge as well the courteous assistance of Dr. Kathleen B. Murphy, Professor of Latin, for advice on the Latin translations; the aid of L. C. and J. E. Tobin for their generous expenditure of time and patience in reading the proofs. I am deeply indebted to the artistic taste of L. Queriman for the selection of the plates, and I express my appreciation of the kind cooperation of the Librarians of the Hispanic Museum and of the Metropolitan Museum in securing these. To all I offer my gratitude. To them be the merits of this book, to me alone the faults.

M. R. M.

Feast of the Holy Guardian Angels,
1929.

LIST OF ILLUSTRATIONS

INTRODUCTION

IT may be inquired, why study Spanish institutions? While the aim of this book is to answer that question, some preliminary remarks on the place of Spain in European history are in order.

There are three great military strategic areas around which have centered the conflicts for the hegemony of Europe, namely the Rhine valley, the Bosphorus and the Straits of Gibraltar. The last two have had a special significance in addition, since by way of them the Arabs and Moslems have threatened and might threaten again the Christian culture established on the ruins of the Roman empire. Hence the possession of these becomes of keenest moment to the problem of European peace, a great point of which is whether one or all of the European nations together, shall hold these positions.

Of all the nations Spain alone has seen this problem clearly in the light of principles of culture rather than of military necessity. It does not seem probable that this is a matter of chance. Rather is the cause to be sought in the position of Spain and in the quality of her culture. Geographically, Spain is a unit, all but thrown off from the continent of Europe, but since the days when the Carthaginians used it as a base against Rome, it has remained within the center of European politics, now dominant, now aloof, sometimes in the background, never unimportant however much it might seem to be such.

Once Romanized, Spain furnished leaders to Rome itself,

leaders of culture and of the art of administration. The Visigothic invasion broke the political links with Rome, but opened the way to a fuller acceptance of the Catholic culture preserved in the strategically situated municipia of Roman administration. Again it produced leaders of culture, as Isidore of Seville and the line of his distinguished disciples. These constructed a Spanish society on the principles outlined by St. Augustine. Though the Arab invasions threatened to ruin this development, step by step the reconstruction won its way until during the reigns of the Catholic Kings, it extended its frontier to Granada. During this period an overflow of Spanish intellectual energy found its way into France and into all Europe which aimed to establish a culture beyond that of barbarism.

Cardinal Ximénez de Cisneros, that remarkable statesman, saw that Granada could not remain the frontier of Spanish Christian culture, and endeavored to spread its influence into Africa, a policy appreciated by the Emperor Charles V, who was an accident in Spain as so many historians are fond of saying. Yet through him the Christian culture of Europe was entrenched on the Rhine and Danube and Europe all but won to its old unity. This could not have been accomplished without the aid of Spain. For a brief pause this country held the key positions on the Scheldt, the Saône and the Po; also strategic outposts of Spanish culture were planted in Mexico, Peru and the Philippines, and *glacis* created from which to launch a conquest of the Oriental peoples.

France, however, looked upon these positions in Europe as strategic points vital to the maintenance of her military hegemony; while England began to see in the New World strategic points from which to shape the commercial hegemony of the world. The two united against Spain in a duel so deadly that as Scelle remarks every moral convention imposed silence as to its real aims.[1] Slowly but surely Spain was driven back to her Iberian base; the Treaties of the Pyrenees, of Aix-la-Chapelle, of Nymwegen, of Utrecht marked the tragic losses, as well as dissensions among her enemies. Owing to these the eighteenth century saw a slight recovery of her fortunes, but the opening of the nineteenth found her soil the decisive battle ground of her greatest rivals. The twentieth century dawned upon a Spain sapped of its energy, holding impregnable only the lonely outpost of her European home and the strategic stretch in Africa from Ceuta to Melilla. Attacks had also been made upon her intellectual culture; it was sneered at, belittled and finally buried behind a wall of silence. Apparently Spain was eliminated from the European scene but the events of the World War reshuffled the cards of politics.

As a result of this war and the diplomatic flounderings since the Treaties of 1919, France now holds the Piedmont passes and the Rhine-Rhône line, from which the shadow of her power falls beyond the Black Forest to Vienna, while southwards it reaches from Paris through Marseilles to Oran and Dakar into South America. This skirts Gibraltar and the Spanish zone in Africa and crosses the British route beyond Gibraltar to Suez and the Far East. This development reveals that once again Spain lies within the heart of European politics where perhaps it will take a part in the approaching crisis when principles of culture and principles of military necessity will clash. This situation was foreshadowed in certain events since the *Entente Cordiale* of 1904. The Conference of Algeciras, the Agadir incident, the Tangier internationalization scheme, the new Italy—all are links in a slowly forming situation. Was it only to capture

[1] *La Traité négrière aux Indes de Castille*, Paris, 1906.

a Moroccan bandit that Spain flung 200,000 and France 100,000 men into Africa? Within the "magic triangle" of Tangier, Ceuta, Gibraltar, Spanish, French, Italian and British interests are entwined and enclose the strategic centers of world peace from both a military and a cultural point of view.

The significance of this new importance of Spain is sensed by thoughtful Europeans, particularly in Germany and France where research in the field of Spanish history has been active. Cirot has made it clear that everything written on the period of Charles V and Philip II must be rewritten from the sources.[2] German historians such as Baumgarten [3] and Häbler [4] and the Spanish Arias y Miranda [5] have started controversies on Spanish economic development which if followed up will force a new criticism of modern economic theory. Spanish historians such as Pérez-Pujol [6] and Hinojosa y Naveros [7] and the Portuguese Gama Barros [8] have pointed the way to a rewriting of the history of Spanish institutions, without the hampering myth of Teutonic superiorities. South American historians are beginning to recover from the nineteenth century Liberal bias and while the United States has not as yet produced an epoch-marking work on Spain, it has a number of sympathetic writers who shine by contrast with the school of Robertson and who have done much to relieve their generation of ancient prejudices. All these but scratch the surface of possibilities, yet already they have presented new points for considera-

[2] Cirot, G.E.A., *Etudes sur l'historiographie espagnole,* Bordeaux, 1905.

[3] Baumgarten, H., *Geschichte Karl V,* 4 vols., Stuttgart, 1886-92.

[4] Häbler, K., *Die Geschichte der Fugger'schen Handlung in Spanien,* Weimar, 1897; *Die Wirtschaftliche Blüte Spaniens im 16 Jahrhundert und ihr Verfall,* Berlin, 1888; *Geschichte Spaniens unter den Hapsburgern,* Gotha, 1907.

[5] Arias y Miranda, J., *Examen crítico histórico del influyo que tuvo en el comercio, industria y población de España su dominación en América,* Madrid, 1854.

[6] Pérez-Pujol, E., *Historia de las Instituciones sociales de la España Goda,* Madrid, 1896.

[7] Hinojosa y Naveros, E. de, *Estudios criticos sobre la Historia del derecho español,* Madrid, 1903.

[8] Gama Barros, H., *Historia da Administraçao Publica em Portugal nos seculos XII a XV,* Lisbon, 1885-1914.

tion in the four major problems of modern Spanish history.

Space does not permit more than a brief mention of them here. The first which comes to mind is what was the real significance to European politics of the reigns of Charles V and Philip II. What were the true aims of these monarchs and why after them did Spain fall so suddenly from the premier place in Europe?

A thousand volumes leaves the mystery as dense as ever. One key to the problem might be found in the study of the trade connections between Ireland, Spain and the Low Countries. The Elizabethan fury in Ireland and the wars in the Low countries have not received their due consideration from historians as yet. A second problem, also economic, the peculiar economic development of Spanish America, still awaits the interpretative historian. Spanish America could and did compete in quality with the European factories but not in cheapness, and hence was forced to export the metals which in turn complicated European trade policies. Economic theories criticizing this situation have been elaborated without adequate study of events in Spain or in reference to Spanish thought on the subject.[9] Hence superficial conclusions have gained currency as valid principles when a proper study of the Spanish sources would have reorientated the whole problem.

A third problem, the sudden fall of Spain, may be studied in the effect this had on the equilibrium of Europe. Since the decline of Spain, Europe has been trying to balance itself from its periphery, England, instead of from its center of gravity, and historians blind to Spanish events have accepted this as normal despite the dreadful wars and the still more dreadful havoc in the intellectual life of Europe which

[9] A recent contribution in this field is Laures, S. J., Rev. J. J., Political Economy of Juan de Mariana, New York, 1928.

it has caused. This problem of politics is closely allied to the fourth great European problem, the control of empire.

To the European world of the sixteenth and seventeenth centuries, Spain dominated because she possessed the Rhine and Italy. Could she have closed the gaps in between, she would then have held the areas dominated of old by Rome. The struggle of France to prevent her came just at the time when the political theory upon which Europe had constructed its system of government was definitely eclipsed by the theories suggested so powerfully by Marsiglio of Padua and Machiavelli. Return to imperial Rome became the fashion of political thought and it was perhaps but natural for observers at a time of confusion and transition to imagine that Spain, wearing the outward dress must also possess the inward soul of old Rome. So magnificent did she appear that envy was aroused, and while her enemies despoiled her, they copied as they thought the model of empire, and strove to dot the world with empires greater than Rome had dreamed of.

But they did not copy Spain, they copied a simulacrum and made mockery of Spanish ideals. Viewing these strange images around her, Spain did not recognize her world and withdrew within herself, while the rest of Europe went on its way, until lately increasing difficulties have forced a backward glance at the mighty vision of Spain. What was this empire which Spain constructed?

Historians are now circling around this question, more or less gingerly, inhibited by old preconceptions. As the criticism of modern empires and the social organization of modern society becomes more and more sharp, it is beginning to go back to earlier medieval systems of government and organization from which to gather point and perspective with the surprising result that the inspirational origins of the most telling institutions are seen to come from medieval Spain. The thought is clearly being voiced that Spain is the mother of European culture, particularly in government and law, those twin institutions within which social character is nourished and supported, and as this study proceeds, the true rôle of Spain emerges from the fogs of myth and misrepresentation.

When read aright her history proves that her periods of "dominance" coincide with those crises when civilization is threatened or in need of reconstruction. It was so after Hannibal, after the invasions of the Arabs, after the discovery of the New World. And she falls back upon herself when her message becomes unintelligible to generations seeking not culture but power.

All signs point to an approaching crisis when civilization must once more be reconstructed if it is to survive. To hold that Spain will rise to assume her historic rôle is to prophesy.

This much may be ventured, and what is said is offered as the justification of this book. The true cause of the special place Spain has occupied in the world, may be traced to the fact that Spanish culture is Catholic culture, and Catholic culture is never so truly Catholic as when it concerns itself with the profound problems of law and government. Hence it is in these fields particularly that Spanish culture can be most profitably studied today. For our generation has clearly lost the meaning of law and cannot find the secret of government.

The unique principles informing the Spanish concept of law and the institutions of the monarchy, the *cortes*, the *municipios*, express a theory of social organization which owes its originality to Catholic thought. It has no military significance whatsoever, though nurtured in the stern school of constant warfare. It was once the patrimony of Europe and Europe robbed of it sinks into ever greater woe. It holds no dream of empire. Ferdinand and Isabella and their grandson, Charles V, did not seek to build empire either in the New World or on the Rhine and Danube. How little the modern world of philosophical historians appreciate this may be judged by their constant incorrect translation of the Spanish term for the possessions beyond the sea. Empire or colonial empire is the preferred term, though neither conveys the meaning of *dominación, posessiones de ultramar* or *dominación española en América.* These should be translated: the Spanish authority or the possessions over which the Spanish authority has jurisdiction. The Spanish connotation of "authority" is hardly imagined by our historians,[10] and it is just this connotation, which when properly understood in the light of its development in Spain, gives the key to Spanish legal thought, and in contrast interprets European history since the Renaissance, explains French ambitions for military security, dissects accurately British ideals of empire and may show Europe the way out of her dilemmas.

The explanation of this term forms the subject matter of this book, and it will be sought in an analysis of the political theory and law as found in the codes of Spain. These are for Castile the Lex Visigothorum or Forum Iudiciorum, the *Fuero Real* and *Las Siete Partidas;* for the eastern kingdoms, the *Usatges* of Barcelona and the *Costumbres* of Tortosa; and the collections of municipal *fueros.* These form the tradition for all Spain and their principles are the subject matter of extended comment in the work of all the great theologian-philosopher-legists such as de Vitoria, Melchior Cano, Domingo de Soto, Mariana, Luis de Molina and Suarez, to mention but the more famous.

It is in the light of this tradition that the last great code,

[10] cf. Merrimam, R.B., Rise of the Spanish Empire, New York, 1918-25, 3 vols.

the *Recopilación de las Leyes de Indías,* must be studied, if it is to be comprehended, and so this book may also be taken as preliminary to its interpretation. It is now generally recognized as one of the famous codes of history. Comment on it, however, has been confined to admiration for its humane provisions, tempered with a lament over the gulf between theory and practice, which is assumed by many historians writing in English to be found as normal in Spanish colonial practice. Criticism grants that it expresses the best that any nation could do under the circumstances, but its detailed clauses have been considered as more or less a natural accompaniment to the quaint times and still quainter views current during its development and final promulgation.

This code drawn up for the government of a subject race and an inferior civilization is far more than this. It is not too much to say that it is the greatest example extant of applied Christian ethics and theology in the field of international law, and as such is a monument of human genius in this difficult sphere.[11]

To couple theology and law appears incongruous to many; so much so that obscurantism or bigotry seem the only fitting terms to apply. But to look to theology for guidance in law making was the natural and logical procedure for the Spaniard of the sixteenth century. To understand this Spanish conception which was the root principle of all their activity in government and political action, one must survey the conditions in which it originated and gave form to the first Spanish state. State is here used advisedly, for though this

---

[11] In *Social Theories of the Middle Ages* (Boston, 1926), Dom Bede Jarrett calls attention to the importance of medieval theories for the student of modern social, political and economic problems. He does not, however, give due weight to the influence of the Augustinian theory upon medieval institutions or to the source of confusion introduced into these by the teachings of the Roman lawyers who became infected with Stoic doctrines from their study of the Roman Justinian law. As a result Dom Bede Jarrett in his turn confuses the true significance of the doctrines of St. Thomas on political theory as a supplement to the Augustinian theory.

term had a connotation quite diverse from the modern sense, it should not be supposed that the medieval Spanish did not have a clear conception of civil society, nor that their political institutions were not broadly planned and comprehensively worked out to allow of a flexible organization,—provided the original principles were kept in view.

The history of institutions is inseparable from the history of ideas, and the source from which the Spanish drew the inspiration for their political ideas may be looked for partly in the Visigothic customs, partly in the Augustinian conceptions of the state and partly in the Politics of Aristotle. But most of all in the philosophy of life presented in the Catholic religion and in the great principles of her theological system. It is to be doubted if Spanish political thought ever quite separated philosophy and theology and when the distinction was attempted, decadence resulted.[12] Nor was this latter due entirely to the fact that the purely philosophical view attempted derived from the Justinian Code and imported French and Italian speculations removed from the Catholic tradition.

From the Forum Iudiciorum, the first code after the III Council of Toledo (and even earlier), these principles were adopted: law and morality are inseparable, and government is applied justice.

Though in these early days such simple realities were considered adequate to compose all the difficulties arising when men attempt to live in civil society, their further elaboration in the course of the centuries never lost touch with them, even when Don Alfonso the Wise asked his Roman lawyers to codify in the Roman style the mass of existing legislation into the great *Las Siete Partidas.* In the sixteenth and seventeenth centuries, the theologians were a unit in

[12] Hinojosa, E. de, *Influencia que tuvieron . . . . los filósofos y teólogos,* Madrid, 1890.

holding that theology was not only the science of God, but also the science of man and reason, and hence also the science of justice and injustice. As de Vitoria said in his "Relectio de Potestate civile", there is nothing foreign to theology.[13] Melchior Cano put theology and civil law together, so also Domingo de Soto, Alfonso de Castro, Santiago de Simancas, Mariana, Luis de Molina and Suarez.[14]

These two conceptions then—law and morality go hand in hand, and justice is the fundamental purpose and aim of civil society—were firmly rooted in the Spanish mind. The Spanish affinity for such principles is variously explained: The reasons may lie in the Spanish temperament, which from Rome received a definite direction towards love of order, and from the barbarians a simple wisdom to accept superior advice. But it may be nothing more than that the Spanish intelligence was gifted with the insight to cling to the truth once presented, though it did not always penetrate to its significance.[15] Not to go into speculations as to the proportions in which the Roman-barbarian elements are blended in the Spanish character, it is certainly true that historical events have deepened the natural tenacity and strong conservatism which distinguished the Iberian peoples even before the days of their Romanization, qualities favorable to building up a strong tradition.

This tradition may be said to have crystallized before the Reconquest and to have prevailed through the tenth, eleventh, twelfth and thirteenth centuries when the outline of the Spanish state is clearly visible. In the main divisions,

---

[13] Hinojosa, ibid., p. 86.

[14] Hinojosa, ibid., pp. 86-98.

[15] Isidore of Seville writes thus of the Goths: a people by nature destructive, of spirited intelligence, restrained by the force of conscience, powerful in the strength of their bodies, eager to develop their bodies, conspicuous in bearing and gesture, quick with their hands, enduring wounds hardily. (Populi natura pernicies, ingenio alacres, conscientiae viribus freti, robore corporis validi, staturae procuritate ardui, gestu habituque conspicui, manu prompti, duri vulneribus. . . Hist. de Rebus Goth. in P. L., vol. 83.

Castile and Aragon, the civil organization was on federal lines, though not federal in the sense of a union of sovereign states as we think of the terms, rather in the sense of a union of sovereign political entities which found their link and natural unity in the person of the sovereign. In Castile, which became typical, these entities took the form of [16]

(a) *Comunidades* or *concejos,* self-governing republics, which raised troops, imposed taxes and administered justice.

(b) *Behetrías,* a special form of republic or *señorio,* which chose for its chief the one who seemed to it best; sometimes of noble lineage, sometimes not; this was known technically as *de mar á mar.*

(c) *Señorios patrimoniales,* a species of hereditary monarchies in which the lord within certain restrictions imposed taxes, collected rents, raised armies and administered justice.

(d) *Señorios* of Bishops and Abbots who were lords of vassals and exercised civil jurisdiction.

In addition the Castilian nobility was a distinct political entity with its *fuero.* This nobility having lost in the course of time its traces of relationship with its predecessor, the Visigothic nobility, assumed this special position owing to the necessities of the Reconquest and struggle with the Moors, circumstances peculiar to Castile.

Each of these entities had its own *fueros* regulating its internal relations, the civil rights of the inhabitants, and their relations with the king, but all looked to him as the fount of all *señorios* and without his confirmation no rights of their class could be created legitimately. Not that they recognized their rights as deriving from him in any way, but because he was considered the regulator of the whole social and political organization, the umpire and the judge in all

[16] Pidal, P. J., in Introductory essay to *Fuero Viejo de Castilla* in *Los Códigos Españoles,* Vol. I, p. 245.

differences in his function of the distributor of justice. He did not give justice, he declared justice, he was the expression of justice.[17] Later this conception changed. Ferdinand de Pulgar speaks of *le Bras du Roi* as if royalty were an estate, like the towns or nobility.[18]

In Spanish political thought from the earliest times, justice was not only the end of human society, it was the norm and method of regulating civil society, and in fact the civil state had no other justification save that through it justice was secured. The state as an entity, either abstract or concrete, to which people owed allegiance and which had rights over the people composing it, never entered into the concept of Spanish legal thinking.[19] Instead they conceived of civil society as a series of more or less connected relations between persons, arising out of the necessities of life here on earth. This life being merely in the way of a sojourn in preparation for the complete life to be lived hereafter, and as such a test of the strength of man, was only conceived of by them in the light of the relations which were held to be necessary, in view of the nature of man, to attaining that end, and hence needed nothing more in the way of organization than was necessary for regulating such relations.

Such an idea may seem odd to the humanitarians of today

---

[17] Mariéjol, *L'Espagne sous Ferdinande et Isabelle,* Paris, 1892, p. 180.

[18] Ibid., p. 135.

[19] It is to be noted that political thinkers have been slow to formulate a definition of the state. The necessity of political rule was seen by Aristotle; the principle of authority was outlined in the Scriptures and developed by many eminent Christian thinkers, such as St. John Chrysostom, St. Augustine and St. Thomas Aquinas. From the teaching of these was constructed the medieval idea of civil society to which Cardinal Bellarmine gave a clear expression in chapters five and six of his De Laicis. In this he points out the twin elements of necessity and the conventional in society. Edmund Burke, grasping the implications of this, perceived that not only has civil society the great purpose of conserving the enjoyment of the natural rights of man, but also it has an existence beyond the mere will of man. From its necessity he deduces the continuity it must have over and above the existing generation. This necessary character of civil society, being "a part of the moral and physical disposition of things," attaches upon every individual in it, certain duties and likewise confers upon the civil society jurisdiction and coercive power. (cf. De Laicis, or the Treatise on Civil Government, tr. K. E. Murphy, Fordham University Press, New York, 1928, pp. 20-30; The History and Development of the Democratic Government in Christian Tradition by Rev. Moorhouse I. X. Millar, S.J., and The End of the State by Rev. John A. Ryan in "The State and the Church," Ryan and Millar, New York, 1922.)

who find the answer to their riddles in an idea of a state more real to them than their neighbor next door, a state which regulates everything as of right. (This latter idea should seem equally odd to those who view the state as an institution with its powers and jurisdictions, rights and duties conditioned by the democratic principles derived from Scholastic philosophy.) The origins of the Scholastic idea may be found in the philosophical and theological ideas developed by St. Augustine in the De Civitate Dei and elsewhere. These found their way into Spanish thought through Orosius who copied Augustine in his Adversum Paganos historianum (completed in 417) and who was used as a source by Isidore of Seville.[20]

This theory of the state as a federal unity of the diverse yet interconnected interests of men, directed and held together by the sovereign who was to be the arbiter to resolve their conflicts and the dispenser of justice which should define the order in which they were to function, is a very interesting attempt to develop what might be called politico-non-sociological conceptions. Original as it is and full of suggestions for the student of the problems of government, this theory is deserving of study.

We may survey the elaboration of the idea through three well-defined periods: the Visigothic kingdom, from the times of the Forum Iudiciorum to the thirteenth century when the influence of the Justinian studies began to be felt, and the introduction of new institutions during the conflict between the Justinian principles and the old Spanish tradition. With

---

[20] Ballester y Castell, R., *Las Fuentes Narrativas de la historia de España durante edad media, 417-1474,* Palma de Mallorca, 1908, pp. 15-6.

Historianum Adversum Paganos, libri vii, ed. Carolus Zangmeister, Vindobonae, 1882, in Vol. V of Corpus Scriptorum ecclesiasticorum Latinorum. Zangmeister shows that Orosius used Augustine 53 times, borrowing from De Civitate, the Confessions and the Letters. He says it is certain (p. xxx) that Isidore, though he does not mention Orosius used him in his De Natura, the Chronicon, the History of the Goths, Suevi and Vandals, and in the Etymologies. (Arevolus quid traditum sit parum indicavit quin etiam Isidorum hic illic ex Orosii editione tacite interpolavit: Otto autem optimos codices mire neclexit.) cf. H. Dressel, De Isidori Orig. fontibus, dissertation at Göttingen, in *Revista de Filol.,* 1874.

the controversies of the sixteenth century and the final form of the *Novíssima Recopilación* of Philip II, the splendid theory of Augustine in its Spanish dress, if it did not succumb entirely, became overlaid almost beyond recognition by the contrary principles of the Justinian law. The Code of the Indies came out just at this critical time.

The problems presented by the discovery of the New World and the existence there of a people whose character and culture were so strange to the European experience of that time, was a tremendous test of the efficiency and efficacy of the Spanish theory. At first glance the necessity of establishing the basis upon which the relationships between the Spanish and the Indian cultures could rest, found in this theory ideal principles of solution. But this century saw the Spanish mind confused as to the meaning of its own tradition, and though it was clear enough yet to plot the outline of the structure of civilization it wished to raise in the New World, it was not clear enough to meet and master the opposition launched suddenly from the four quarters of Europe. Islamism, defeated in Spain, won on the Danube; Stoicism, silenced, became vocal again from Bologna and Paris, and found more powerful allies than ever in the national states that contested with Spain for the prize of the Indies. Spain's experiment was shattered; Mexico, the loveliest jewel fashioned from her theory in the New World, became the theatre of the fiercest struggle. The battle is still drawn, the issue not yet concluded.

Is the theory still valid? From a study of it lessons may be drawn to point the moral of this struggle, and furnish the principles upon which the issue may lead to peace.

This last question is difficult and far-reaching, and the answer will not be attempted here. But by describing the ideas involved in the theory, tracing their development, and illustrating some of their applications in the institutions set up, it is hoped that this essay may suggest the lines along which investigation should be carried if progress is to be made.

Part I

PRINCIPLES OF THE THEORY

La ley es por demostrar las cosas de Dios é que desmuestra bien bevir y es fuente de disciplina é que muestra el derecho é faze é que ordena las buenas costumbres, é govierna la cibdad é ama justicia, y es maestra de vertudes é vida de todo el pueblo.

Fuero Juzgo, Lib. I, *Tít.* II, *ley* 2.

SAINT ISIDORE OF SEVILLE

Chapter I

Doctrines of St. Isidore of Seville which Influenced Spanish Legal Thought

IN St. Isidore of Seville, *el Doctor de Españas,* Spain found the writer to express those principles which became the basis of her philosophy of government. That St. Isidore was her master in this, was due to his broad culture, his power of synthesis, his clearness of exposition, and the genius, almost, which made him not only the towering figure of his own generation, but for many generations after him, both in and beyond Spain. Through him were transmitted the old Graeco-Roman-Spanish culture and the new legal principles introduced into the world by the Catholic Church.

It is an error, fast becoming a vulgar error, to imagine that the Church as such sought to impose a culture upon the Spanish people which later developed into some kind of a hybrid called a Theocratic State, or a State-Church, or a Church-State, according to the particular historian's fancy. Those who read Spanish history, especially Spanish legal history, with this conception, are bound never to make anything of it but a muddle. Spanish culture, it is true, became Catholic culture, but this resulted from the natural course of events and the influence of a religion which contains in itself the principles of life. As a living force, it modified ideas and institutions, and would have done so independently of any expressed policy or purpose.

Once Roman rule was established in Spain, Roman institutions and Roman customs were accepted by the people, though the old Celtiberian ideas were never entirely obliterated. Christianity took root in Apostolic times and by the third century, the ecclesiastical hierarchy and Catholic life were fully established. The chief interest of the Church during this period was to extend religion, consolidate the disciples and develop Catholic teaching as the needs of the pagan society and the nascent heresies demanded. The canons of the Councils, national, provincial or diocesan, anterior to the third Council of Toledo, are confined to prohibiting contact between the Christians and the pagans and to safeguarding the Catholic life amid the mass of pagan customs and ways.[1] Though owing to the persecutions, these could not be summoned regularly, they formed an ecclesiastical tribunal of great importance in the life of the Church and the center from which radiated her activity. As both clergy and people elected the bishops, the government of the Church had a democratic significance, which made the bishops the most genuine representatives of the necessities and aspirations of society.[2] By the fourth century monastic life was also common in Spain.

During the later Roman empire, society was fast crystallizing into castes, and the clergy formed somewhat of a class apart, with certain privileges and immunities, deriving partly from the precedents set by the position of the Hebrews in the empire, partly by the pagan traditions for the treatment of the ministers of religion, and partly from the policy of Constantine. Spanish practice followed that of the Empire. The influence accrued to the clergy by these circumstances helped to ameliorate the unhappy conditions of pagan society, and in the canons of the Council of Iliberis,

[1] Pérez-Pujol, *Historia de las Instituciones Sociales de la España-Goda*, Madrid, 1896, I, p. 385. The acts of the Council of Iliberis, held around 300, are the earliest preserved. For texts of this and others of this period, such as Concilium Taragonense, Gerundense, Valletanum, see Migne, P.L., vol. 84.

[2] Pérez-Pujol, op cit., I, p. 387.

may be seen what evils were attacked,—immorality, usury, excessive punishment of slaves, the shows of the circus and the theatres, libels against the Church, the pest of informers and false witnesses, etc. The action of Christianity, while slowly modifying the principles of the Roman law, could not reconstruct the enfeebled Roman society of the fourth century, and in Spain this century reflected the decadence everywhere visible in the Empire. Nor did the Christians escape. Though there were notable exceptions like Paciano of Barcelona and Asturio and Petrunio (praised by St. Ildefonsus and St. Geronimus), the general level was low. The canons of the first Council of Saragossa (380) and of Toledo (400) reveal a deterioration not found in the third century.

In the fifth century came the sweep of the barbarian invasions, the Vandals settling in Lusitania, the Suevi in Betica, the Alani in Galicia. The sections around Tarragona and Cartagena and to the east remained Roman. Then the Goths inundated the land, gradually extending their sway over the other peoples. Under Theodoric the court was fixed at Toledo, agriculture was revived, and the country may be said to have settled down to ways of peace unknown since the days of the first invasions, according to Isidore of Seville.

Though the Goths might be called the Greeks of the barbarians, they were still barbarians. Their state rested on conquest, and in the alteration of institutions that followed, force predominated over thought, military over the scientific and cultural elements, barbarian customs over those of the cultivated Latins. Philosophy, oratory, all that the Romans called disciplinae or artes liberales, fell rapidly into decay, since they served neither the efficiency of the individual, nor for the direction of the destinies of the State in the new order of society. The old schools of the Romans disappeared and such famous centers of learning as Tarragona, Cartagena, Seville, Lérida and Braga declined.[3]

The church too had established seminaries for the education of the clergy, and also for secular learning in order to combat the pagan philosophies of the times.[4] Such schools flourished in Spain on the same models, and this organization was preserved until the fall of the Gothic monarchy in the monastic and cathedral schools. We have mention of a primary school in the monastery of Carliana, some twelve kilometers from Lérida, and no doubt the greater part of the monasteries and convents had similar schools.[5]

The importance which the Church had acquired among the Goths, especially after the abjuration of Arianism, was due in great part to just this fact that the clergy had the only schools in which the aristocratic Goths, more devoted to culture than the other barbarians, could be educated. These schools alone preserved the knowledge of Graeco-Roman culture. The clergy too had the only prestige left in the old society, partly because of the errors committed by the imperial civil administration in crushing the middle class and in weakening the municipia, and partly because the bishops as the only responsible officials left, took over the charge of the common property of the municipia and practically the whole of the civil administration as well. Amid the unstable conditions of the barbarian kingdoms it was impera-

[3] In 506 the *Brevario* of Alaric omits all the titles and laws of the Theodosian code relative to students, professors and education (Pérez-Pujol, op. cit., III, p. 491 and note 1). Roman culture first took root in Betica, the Tudetani being more docile and more cultured than the rest of Spain, on account of the greater influence of Phoenician and Greek learning. Seville was the chief city of Betica (see Cañal, C., *San Isidoro*, Seville, 1897, p. 25).

[4] Such importance had these schools assumed and such influence through the secular learning were the principles of Christianity gaining over the people, that Julian the Apostate withdrew from the municipia, the rights which they had enjoyed of naming professors and opening schools (Cod. Theod., lib. xiii, tit. ii, lex 5, quoted in Pérez-Pujol, III, p. 461, note 3 and also note 4, quotation from Ammiano Marcelino, Rerum Gestarum).

[5] Pérez-Pujol, III, p. 493, also pp. 505-80. The lay schools of the Roman municipia were not revived. For an account of the higher education, cf. the Etymologies of Isidore and Bourret, J.R., *L'Ecole chrétienne de Seville sous la monarchie des Visigoths*, Paris, 1855.

tive for the Goths if they were to rule, to secure the aid of such experienced and powerful forces.[6]

The Catholic society as such, however, did not exercise any influence on the laws and political institutions from Ataulf to Leovigild. Persecuted by some monarchs as Euric, tolerated by others, they lacked the means to do much, but with Reccared and the third Council of Toledo began a new situation in which the clergy could act. The lesson of the heroic resistance of the Catholic populations to the attempts of Leovigild to Arianize them was not lost, and if the Goths were to hold their own against French and Byzantine effort, unity was essential. The greater part of the population was Catholic and Reccared yielded to the logic of facts and surrendered.

The leaders of the Catholic clergy during these times were Saints Braulio, Julian, Ildefonso, Eugenio, Pablo el Emeritense, Maximo, Conancio, Tajón and Valerio.[7] The method chosen by the clergy to spread Christian principles was not through political action, but through the schools. The most noted of the monastic schools were those of Dumiense, Maximo, Asaniense, Servitano and Agaliense.[8] The episcopal schools owed their beginning to the second Council of Toledo (527), canon I, but remained in rudimentary form until St. Leandro, in imitation of the schools created by St. Augustine and his disciples in Africa, opened schools for the youth of Seville.[9] St. Leandro, Archbishop of Seville in 579, was obliged to take refuge in Constantinople during the persecutions of Leovigild, and there picked up the best of Byzantine culture and became the friend of St. Gregory the

[6] Reccared invited the bishops to take seats in the Assemblies and Councils, Hinojosa, *Influencia que tuvieron . . . . . los filósofos y teólogos,* p. 23.
[7] Cañal, C. *San Isidoro,* p. 23.
[8] La Fuente, M. de, *Historia General de España,* Barcelona, 1889, II, p. 112.
[9] Cañal, C., *Sevilla prehistorica,* Seville, 1894.

Great. He returned to Spain under Reccared and took a leading part in his conversion. His greatest service was the school at Seville from which his disciples spread the Catholic Faith and established similar schools at Toledo, Saragossa, Braga and other places.[10]

Of his three brothers, Fulgencio, Florentino (who became the first Christian poet of Spain), and Severino, the last became famous as the father of St. Isidore (d. 636). Educated by his uncles, Leandro and Florentino, Isidore was early noted for his learning. Among his works, the Sentenciae [11] and the *Etimologias* [12] are the chief sources for his juridical principles, and he himself is the channel for the transmission of the Catholic tradition which was to dominate Spanish legal thought and that of the greater part of Europe.[13]

His great contribution is to be found in the theories on authority, the criterion for good government and the social

---

[10] Cañal, C., *San Isidoro,* p. 27.

[11] This, the most important of his dogmatic works, is in three parts and forms the transition from the Fathers to Scholasticism, in the opinion of Menéndez y Pelayo (*La Ciencia española,* III; *Hist. de las ideas estet.,* VI, pp. 346-349). His sources are Augustine, Plato, Aristotle (from his uncle's teaching) and Gregory the Great. The translation of the Sentenciae made for Peter Lombard was one of the first monuments of German prose (Cañal, *San Isidoro,* p. 115).

[12] The division of these into twenty books was made by his disciple, St. Braulio of Saragossa (Cañal, p. 68). Isidore used them as a text book in his classes at Seville, where he organized the curriculum.

[13] In the ninth century, his views on the nature of the state and its relation with the Church were respected and held in the Councils of Frankfurt-am-Main, 794, where his doctrines in Lib. viii, c. vii of the *Etimologias* were quoted against the errors of Felix and Elipando; of Aquisgran II, 836; of Maguncia, 888. In the last three, the doctrines on the king, his duties, and relations with the Church are developed from the *Etimologias* and the Sentenciae. The manuscripts of his follower, Tajón, may be found in Paris and Normandy, and German and Italian monks came to the Spain of the Reconquest to copy the works of Leandro, Isidore, Braulio of Saragossa and Ildefonso. In the empire of Charlemagne, three distinguished students of his tradition, Teodulfo, Bishop of Orléans, Claudio, Bishop of Turin, and Prudencio Galindo, the poet-Bishop of Troyes, took a leading part in the renaissance of culture. Another famous student of Isidore was Gerbert, who was trained under the patronage of the Count of Barcelona, Borrell II, and became Pope Sylvester II (Pérez-Pujol, III, pp. 578-80). Though culture rather declined in Spain during the wars of the Reconquest, there was a revival of the study of Isidore under Don Alfonso VIII and in the famous school of Toledo founded by Archbishop Raimundo, the Archdeacon Domingo Gonzales wrote the treatise De unitate, using the tradition of Isidore. Don Alfonso X ordered a Spanish translation of the *Etimologias,* and borrowed from Isidore when he wrote his *Crónica general* or *Estoria de Espanna.* All during the fourteenth and fifteenth centuries, Isidore is quoted frequently (Cañal, *San Isidoro,* p. 123).

mission of the clergy. The doctrines on these points may be summed up as follows:

(1) Authority comes from God and is instituted by Him for His people.[14] Authority is not something arbitrary, a mere ruling, but a power that coming from God, must be used to His own ends, and thus those exercising it may be held up to a standard. It was understood by this Christian society that the "ends" of God were embraced in a final end, Justice. From this principle was deduced the concept of kingship as the means for securing and directing justice, which we shall find later in the codes.

(2) The criterion for good government was the happiness of the subject,[15] the defense of the Church,[16] and the

---

[14] As the Apostle says, there is no power but from God, as the Lord says through the prophet concerning certain powers, 'They shall reign, but not through Me.' As if He would say, not through My approval but rather through My extreme anger. Whence further on through the same prophet He added, I will give you, He says, a king in My anger. By which He makes more manifest that both good and evil power are ordained by God, but good with his approval, and evil through His anger. When kings are good, it is to be attributed to the beneficence of God, but when they are evil, to the wickedness of the people. That power is good, which comes as a gift from God. (Dum Apostolus dicat: non est potestas nisi a Deo, Rom. xiii, 1, quomodo Dominus per prophetam de quibusdam potestatibus dicit: Ipsi regnaverunt, sed non ex me, Osee, viii, 4. Quasi diceret, non me propitio, sed etiam summe irato. Unde et inferius per eundam prophetam addidit: Dabo, inquit, tibi regem in furore meo, Osee, xiii, 11. Quo manifestius elucet bonam malamque potestatem a Deo ordinari sed bonam propitio, malam irato, Lib. Sent. lib. III, cap. xlviii, 10 in P. L., vol. 83. Reges quando boni sunt muneris est Dei, quando vero mali, sceleris est populi, Ibid., 11. Potestas bona est, quae a Deo donante est, Ibid., 5).

[15] Every mark of power is not thereby advantageous, but it is advantageous, if it is properly used. But it is properly used when it benefits the subjects on whose behalf it is adorned with earthly honor (Non statim utile est omne potestatis insigne, sed tunc vere est utile, si bene geratur. Tunc autem bene geritur quando subiectis prodest, quibus terreno honore praefertur. Lib. Sent., lib. III, cap. xlviii).

God gives to princes the supreme power for the ruling of the people, and he wishes those men to reign over them since for them there is one condition of birth and of death. Therefore rulership should benefit the people, not harm them; nor should the ruler oppress them by domineering but should care for them benignantly in order that this mark of power may be truly beneficial and that they may use this gift of God for the protection of the members of Christ. Indeed the members of Christ are the faithful people; when these rule fittingly with that power which they receive they return by a fitting exchange to God the giver (Dedit Deus principibus praesulatum pro regimine populorum et illis eos praeesse voluit, cum quibus una est, eis nascendi moriendique conditio. Prodesse ergo debet populis principatus, nec nocere; nec dominando premere sed condescendendo consulere; ut vere sit utile hoc potestatis insigne et dono Dei protectione utantur membrorum Christi fidelis sunt populi, quos dum ea potestate quam accipiunt optime regunt bonam utique vicissitudinem Deo largitori restituunt. Lib. Sent. lib. II, cap. xlix, 3).

[16] Let earthly princes know that they ought to give an accounting to God for the Church which they receive from Christ to be cared for, for whether peace and the discipline of the Church are increased by faithful princes or not, He Who entrusted His Church to their power will exact an accounting from them (Cognoscant principes saeculi Deo debere se rationem reddere propter Ecclesiam, quam a Christo tuendam suscipiunt, nam sive augeatur pax, et disciplina Ecclesiae per fideles principes, sive solvatur: ille

just rule of princes, subject not only to the eternal norm of the moral law but also to laws which they themselves promulgate.[17]

(3) In the social mission of the clergy we find the concrete expression of the relations between the Church and the State. Isidore scores those prelates who through fear of losing the favor of princes fail to defend the rights of the people, or to censure those who are oppressing them, and reminds them that the priest of God should always have solicitude for the flock of Christ.[18] We find this same idea expressed in the third Council of Toledo,[19] in the fourth Council of Toledo [20] and in the Fuero Juzgo.[21] So deeply was

---

ab eis rationem exiget, qui eorum potestati suam Ecclesiam credit. Lib. Sent. III, cap. li, 6).

Earthly princes sometimes hold a position of power in the Church, in order that they may defend, through this same power, ecclesiastical discipline (Principes saeculi nonunquam intra Ecclesiam potestatis adeptae culmina tenent ut per eamdem potestatem disciplinam ecclesiasticam muniant, Ibid).

[17] He who makes a right use of the kingly power ought to bear himself before others so that the more brightly his honor shines before men so much the more should he humble himself interiorly (Qui recte utitur regni potestate ita se praestare omnibus debet, ut quanto magis honoris celsitudine claret, tanto semetipsum mente humiliet. Lib. Sent. lib. III, cap. xlix, 1).

He who makes a right use of the kingly power determines the form of justice more by deeds than by words. He is puffed up by no prosperity and cast down by no adversity. He does not trust in his own strength, nor does he forsake the Lord. His heart presides with humble spirit in the highest post of his kingdom. Iniquity does not delight him, nor does the desire for domination inflame him. He makes a poor man rich without defrauding anyone, and what he can obtain from the people by just authority, his mercy often donates to the wretched (Qui recte utitur regni potestate formam iustitiae, factis magis quam verbis instituit. Iste nulla prosperitate erigitur, nulla adversitate turbatur; non innitur proprius viribus, nec Domino recedit cor eius regni fastigio humili praesidet animo; non eum delectat iniquitas non inflammat cupiditas; sine defraudatione alicuius ex paupere divitem facit; et quod iusta potestate a populis extorquere poterat, saepe miseri cordi clementia donat. Ibid. 2).

It is easier for a good king to turn from evil ways to justice than to be led aside from justice to sin, that you may know that it is chance in the latter case but design in the former. His intention should be never to depart from the truth, but if by chance he happen to slip he will soon arise (Bonus rex facilius ad iustitiam a delicto regreditur, quam de iustitia ad delictum transfertur ut noveris hic esse casum, illic propositum. In proposito eius esse debet nunquam egredi a veritate. Quod si casu titubare contigerit, mox resurgere. Ibid. 4).

It is just for a prince to obey his own laws, for he will consider that they should be kept by all when he himself shows reverence for them (Iustum est principum legibus obtemperare suis. Tunc enim iura sua et omnibus custodienda existimet quando et ipse illis reverentiam praebet. Lib. Sent. lib. III, cap. li, 1).

Princes are bound by their own laws, nor can they justly dispense themselves from what they decree for their subjects. For it is just that what they prohibit to the people by the authority of their voice, they should not be allowed to grant to themselves. (Principes legibus teneri suis neque in se posse damnare quae in subiectis constituunt, Iusta est enim vocis eorum auctoritate si quod populis prohibent sibi licere non patiantur. Ibid.)

[18] Lib. Sent. lib. III, cap. xlv, cap. lvii.

[19] Canon xviii. For text see ed. Simonet, F.J., *El III Conciilio de Toledo*, Madrid, 1891.

[20] Canon xxxii. For text of this see P. L., vol. 84.

[21] Lib. II, Titulo I, ley xxviii, according to the Spanish text in *Los Códigos Españoles*, I.

this duty of the clergy fixed in the minds of the Spanish, that it became second nature for them to look to the clergy for criticism and advice.

In the definitions and exposition of the term law, however, we find Isidore's greatest contribution to the science of government. He devotes the fifth book of his Etymologies to its development, though in the second book, chapters ten and eleven, he has some further notes.[22] But as his ideas furnished the groundwork of Spanish thought on this subject, we shall consider them in the discussion on the Lex Visigothorum, where they find their most complete and direct bearing.[23]

We advise the bishops of God that they should watch over the poor and over the unfortunates by the command of God, and they should admonish the judges who judge unjustly against the people that they may improve and follow the good way. They should see to the removal of those who judge wrongly. If these do not wish to do as they are advised and prefer to judge unjustly, the bishop under whose jurisdiction it is, ought to summon the judge so that the other bishops and other good men may declare that he judged unjustly and the bishop with the judge may hear the lawsuit according as is right. And if the judge is so obstinate as not to wish to correct the judgment, the bishop may judge it by himself, and the judgment which was corrected he shall put in writing as it was amended and shall forward it with that which was wrong to the king. The king shall confirm it as it corresponds to what is just. If the judge is to rectify before the bishop all that which before was wrong because of his not going before the bishop, he must pay as a fine to the king, two *libras doro* (Nos amonestamos á los obispos de Diós que deven aver guarda sobre los pobres é sobre los coytados por mandado de Diós, que ellos amonesten los iuzes que iudgan tuerto contra los pueblos que meioren e que fagan buena vía, é que desfagan lo que iudgaron mal. E si ellos non los quisieren fazer por su amonestamiento, é quisieren iudgar tuerto el obispo en cuya tierra es, deve lamar al iuez que dizien que iudgó tuerto é otros obispos é otros omes buenos y emendar el pleyto el obispo cum el iuez segund cuemo es derecho. E si el iuez es tan porfiado que non quiere emendar el iuyzio con él estonze el obispo por lo puede iudgar por sí. Y el iuyzio que fue emendado faga ende un escripto de cuemo lo emendó y enire el escripto con aquel que era agraviado ante el rey, que el rey confirme lo quel semeirare que es derecho. E si el iuez tollier al obispo aquel omne que ante era agraviado por el iuez con tuerto que non venga antel obispo, peche el iuez dos libras doro al rey).

22 The Latin text of the Etymologies may be found in P.L., vol. 82. The sources for his ideas are considered to be the Breviarum Alaricanum, the Theodosian code, the text books of Gaius and Ulpian, the Sententiae of Paulus and Orosius. In Migne may be found mention of Paulus and the Theodosian code.

Joseph Tardif: *Un Abrégé juridique des Etymologies d'Isidore de Séville* in *Mélanges Julien Havet*, Paris, 1895, gives an interesting compilation of the De Legibus in question and answer form from a manuscript edited probably by a cleric in one of the schools of grammar in the north of France, and dating from the early part of the ninth century. It is more from the point of view of the grammarian than that of the jurist, but is valuable as showing how the ideas of Isidore passed into European thought.

The first printed edition of the Etymologies appeared at Augsburg, 1472. The complete works of Isidore were published at Paris, 1580, 1599, 1601, 1778, Cologne, 1617. Migne prints the edition of Arevolo (Rome, 1797-1803). The best recent edition of the Etymologies is that of Lindemann, which forms part of the Corpus Lat. Scrip. printed in Germany towards the middle of nineteenth century.

23 See Chapter III of this essay.

Chapter II

The Lex Visigothorum or the Forum Iudiciorum

THE Lex Visigothorum is called the Liber Iudiciorum in the most ancient codex, that of the Vatican of the eighth century (Vaticanus Reginae Christinae, 1024).[1] It is also called the Liber Iudicum, Liber iudicis, Liber Goticum, Liber legum Gothorum. The name Forum Iudicum is found in the Codex Escurialense of the twelfth century and is used by the Spanish Academy in its edition, Madrid, 1815, as the Latin of the phrase *Fuero Juzgo.*[2]

The Liber Iudiciorum or *Fuero Juzgo* is not, strictly speaking, a code at all, but a compilation of principles for

[1] Ureña y Smenjaud, Rafael de, *La Legislación Gótico-Hispana,* Madrid, 1905, p. 45.

[2] For a learned account of the literature published during the nineteenth century on the Liber Iudiciorum and the Leges Antiquiores and texts of these, see Ureña y Smenjaud, loc. cit., pp. 5-24. Also *Historica Crítica de la literatura española,* Madrid, 1897, by the same author. Thirteen editions of the Liber Iudiciorum have appeared. The first, under the title Codex legum Wisigothorum, by Pedro Pithou, appeared at Paris, 1597, and the last, the critical edition of Zeumer, may be found in Mon. Germ. Hist., Vol. I, Hanover and Leipzig, 1902. This edition sums up the work of German scholarship of the nineteenth century and is authoritative, save for the omission of the Primus Titulus, De Electione principum, and the Placitum directed by the Jews to Chintila (for text of this see Ureña y Smenjaud, pp. 570-75). Zeumer did not give sufficient attention to the Spanish codices and relied too confidingly on the editions of Walther and the Spanish Academy. It contains three versions of the Liber Iudiciorum, the Lex Reccessvindiana, the Lex Evigiana, and the Vulgata. Walther's edition (in his Corpus iuris Germanici antiqui, Berlin, 1824) is the eighth, but Ureña y Smenjaud considers it careless and second hand, following mostly the text of the Spanish Academy edition which is the seventh. This edition, undertaken in 1784, was finally published in Latin and Spanish at Madrid, 1815 and for the first time has the Primus Titulus, De Electione principum, taken from the Codices Complutense and *San Juan de los Reyes.* The editors of this edition were not acquainted with the texts and editions in foreign libraries, particularly in Paris, and ignored several versions in Spain, but despite these faults they made the first attempt in the way of a critical edition (Ureña y Smenjaud, pp. 65, 80). The ninth edition called *La Publicidad,* appeared under the title of *Los Códigos españoles concordados y anotados,* Madrid, 1847—, also called that of Rivadeneyra. A second edition of this came out in 1872-73. The Liber Iudiciorum may be found in Volume I of each edition. In the first edition of this the Latin text is from the version of the Spanish Academy, but unfortunately it suppressed all the notes and is therefore of little use. The Spanish version, under the title, *Fuero Juzgo,* is from the thirteenth century, which was issued at the order of Don Ferdinand III, April 4, 1241, as the *Libro de los Jueces.* There are variations between the Latin and this version.

the use and application of the tribunals of justice. The public Visigothic law is incorporated into it only when the exigencies of practical judgment demand it.[3] To the jurists belong the greater part of the rubrics found at the beginning of each capitulum.[4] It could hardly be otherwise as the Spanish concept of law was quite different from that of today, and needed no codes in the modern sense.

The most important part of the Liber Iudiciorum from the point of view of legal philosophy is the Primus Titulus, De Electione principum, and Book I containing the titles on the Legislator and the Law.[5] These form what might be called the constitution of the Toledan monarchy and the tradition of the Spanish state. But to appreciate the importance

---

[3] Ureña y Smenjaud, p. 450.

[4] Ureña y Smenjaud, p. 462.

[5] The title De Electione principum, based on the Councils of Toledo and the Etymologies of Isidore of Seville, is found only in the seventh edition, that of the Spanish Academy, and the ninth based on this. Ureña y Smenjaud considers this to be a compilation made in the Lex revisa of Ervigio by his successor Egica or perhaps by Egica and Witiza, between 695 or 698 and 702. This was so near to the end of the Gothic monarchy that it explains why it was left out of so many manuscripts by the copyists (Idem., p. 116 and on pp. 136 and 525 may be found a table of the chapters of this title with their origins in the various Toledan councils). In the Codices Complutense and *San Juan de los Reyes,* used by the Spanish Academy and also the Codex Escurialense 2, appear the eighteen chapters of the De Electione principum by themselves, divided into three titles. Some codex of the tenth or beginning of the eleventh century, had these titles on the first sheet of an index to Book I of the Liber Iudiciorum, and this sheet was added, when or by whom is unknown, to the Codex Legionense. On this sheet, stuck to the next one, as if to mend it, and written by a contemporary hand, or perhaps one anterior, to that in which the Codex was copied, may be read as follows:

	I. Tit. De electione principum et eorum adquisita.
De	II. Tit. De reprobatione personarum adipiscere regnum.
Instrumentis legalibus	III. Tit. De commotione principum.
Liber I	IV. Tit. De Legisatore.
	V. Tit. De Lege.

On the Codex Complutense, the three titles are enclosed with the following words written on the margin of the sheet, Incipit Liber primum. Possibly Egica ordered the incorporation of these in Liber I in the form found in the Codex Legionense, and the greater number of the copyists placed it at the beginning of their manuscripts not realizing that the sheet was stuck to the other, and those who came after them limited themselves to copying exactly the little collection. In this way it grew into the preliminary title of the Spanish Academy edition, but Walther and Zeumer omitted it as not belonging to the Liber Iudiciorum proper.

However, the fragment on the Codex Legionense represents in all its purity the addition of Egica (Idem., p. 528). The Complutense, *San Juan de los Reyes* and Escurialense 2, are exact and faithful transcriptions of first copyists, and the manuscripts Matritense 772 and 12924 of the sixteenth century, copy the old tripartite classification. These four codices were utilized by the Spanish Academy. The last two have one more chapter, the De Successione regum (text of which may be found in Appendix a 1 of Ureña y Smenjaud). The manuscript 772 calls it the nineteenth chapter. It is taken from canon xvii of the sixth Council of Toledo and is drawn from the Etymologies.

There is no critical edition of the Titulus, De electione principum, as yet, hence that of the Spanish Academy must be accepted as definite. For discussion of the texts of this title, see Ureña y Smenjaud, pp. 517-27.

of these principles, a little knowledge of the development of the Liber Iudiciorum is of value.

According to Isidore of Seville, the origins of this code go back to Euric,[6] but before him the customary laws of the Goths, called *Belagines* (law, ordinance, mandate or institution) reflected the teaching of Dicineus, a wise teacher of the first century before Christ.[7] In the fourth century, about 377, according to Isidore, through the Arian Ulfilas Christian principles were introduced. During the third and fourth centuries, though the struggle was constant between the Goths and the Romans, little by little the superior Roman culture began to filter into barbarian life, especially by way of the army. Codes were being formed, and according to the testimony of Sidonius Apollinaris, writing between 469-71 during the reign of Euric, there existed the Leges Theodoricianae, drawn up by the Roman jurists. The two Theodorics [8] had their kingdom around Tolosa (Toulouse) as their capital, but Euric was the first to establish the Gothic power in Spain, and therefore could be considered the first legislator of the Gothic-Spanish monarchy.[9]

Fourteen fragments of the Leges Theodoricianae consisting of capitula VII-XX of the first part of a collection of Roman and Gothic laws, exist, made probably in Gaul [10] or in Italy according to Gaudenzi, at the end of the ninth or beginning of the tenth century. These fragments relate to the rights of succession, juridical procedure, donations, interest, sale of a free man, slaves and tribute. They are the remains of an ancient Gothic code as seems clear from the

---

[6] Hist. de Rebus Goth. cap. 35, edition of Arévalo: Sub hoc rege, Gothi legum statuta in scriptis habere coeperunt, nam antea tantum moribus et consuetudine tenebantur.

[7] Ureña y Smenjaud, pp. 171-4.

[8] Called in the Cronica Regum Visigothorum, Theodoricus, in Spain usually Teodoredo.

[9] For a discussion of these laws of Theodoric, see Ureña y Smenjaud, pp. 170-235. For texts, see Zeumer.

[10] Provence, according to Conrat, in *Gesch. der Quellen und Lib. des roms Recht*, pp. 281-4.

barbarian Latin and simple statement of rule and its sanction, but not a code in the strict sense, more nearly an edict divided into chapters and promulgated by a Gothic king in the style of Theodoric the Great, and dating from the fifth century. This edict was from the time of Theodoric II (453-67) and is contained in the Codex rescriptus Parisiensis of the ninth century, and represents the first step in the development of the Liber Iudiciorum. It is referred to in the version of Recceswinth and following ones as the Antiqua.[11]

Euric (467-85), developing the plans and ambitions of Theodoric, extended his sway through Gaul, and in Spain divided his power with the Suevi. He entrusted to his minister, the Gallo-Roman jurist, Leon of Narbonne, the formulation of a national code, the Statuta legum mentioned by Isidore, whose youth was passed under the legal régime of Euric and the Codex revisus of Leovigild. He had these in mind when he wrote his history. One hundred and fifteen of the three hundred and nineteen laws with the heading Antiqua and without title in the Liber Iudiciorum of Recceswinth represent these codes and also the laws of the Gothic peoples. But among the Romanized subjects of the Visigoths in Spain there were in use the Theodosian code (438), the Gregorian and Hermogenianum Corpus (295?, 365?) and the Novellae leges, called the post-Theodosian (447-68). Along with these went the commentaries on the Roman law, such as those of Ulpian and Gaius, the Escolias or Antiqua Summaria codicis Theodosiani, the Interpretationes, the Vaticana fragmenta and the Consultatio veteris cuiusdam iurisconsultus.

Hence Alaric II (485-507) wished to have a compendium

[11] The Antiqua of the Liber Iudiciorum refers to these old laws which are from the Romanized Goths by way of the Theodosian code and what survived of their customary law.

of the laws in force in his Gothic-Gallo-Spanish state, and on February 2, 506, promulgated his Liber Legum, more commonly known as the Lex Romana Visigothorum or the Breviarum Alarici Regis. A commission of jurists, Gallo-Romans, drew up the code according to the ius of the Theodosian code which was approved at Arduis (Aire sur l'Adour) by an assembly of bishops and provincials chosen by the king, according to Hinojosa, or by the people according to Marichalar y Manrique. It was promulgated at Toulouse and the original deposited in the royal treasury. Copies, certified by Aniano, chancellor of the kingdom, were transmitted to the *condes* for immediate use. Many names have been applied to this code, but the most common is the Lex Romana or Lex Romana Visigothorum. The title Breviarum Alarici did not appear until the sixteenth century. The historians speak of it as the Breviarum Aniani. It is a compilation of the chief juridical monuments of the Roman law in force in Spain and in Gaul at the end of the fifth and the beginning of the sixth century. In addition to the sources mentioned above, the Sententiarum Libri V of Paulus and a fragment of Liber I of the Responsorum of Papinius were used. For the interpretation appearing at the side of the text, two theories of its origin are current. Savigny held that it was written by the jurists of Alaric; or it was the work of a Romanist of the fifth century and was used by the editors of the Edict of the Ostrogoth Theodoric the Great.[12]

Thus the two codes—the Statuta legum of Euric and the Lex Romana of Alaric—existed side by side. But as the Gothic sway weakened the attraction of the Roman administration over the Celtiberian peoples, whose customs reap-

[12] Ureña y Smenjaud gives the following authorities for this: Haenel, Antiqua summaria codicis Theodosiani ex codice Vaticano nunc primus edito, Leipzig, 1834; Mon. Ger. Hist. III, p. 580; Dernberg, *Die sogenante Westgothische Interpretatio* in *Zeit. für Rechtsgesch.*, XI, pp. 222-49; Lecrivain, *Rémarques sur l'Interpretation de la Lex Romana Visigothorum*, Toulouse, 1899.

pearing found points of affinity with the Gothic laws, a new impetus was given to making Gothic legislation supreme.[13] In 546 Teudo ordered the addition of a new constitution on the costs and expenses of trials from the Theodosian code, and prepared the way for the revisions of Leovigild which came about 572-86. This established the territorial law over the personal.

This revision provoked a new series of royal constitutions which increased the prestige of the territorial law under Reccared, Sisebut and Chindaswinth. The outstanding act of Reccared was the abjuration of Arianism for the Gothic peoples in the Third Council of Toledo. It created a radical change in the Toledan monarchy. Of course Christian principles had been impregnating Gothic ideas since the time of Ulfilas, and the canon law had been going through a parallel process of development. The Statuta legum of Euric regulated the alienation and possession of ecclesiastical property, and the Antiqua "Nulla de ecclesia" established the principle of immunity of churches and the right of asylum. The Gothic monarchy was essentially military. Now under the influence of the abjuration of the Arian heresy and the Third Council of Toledo, it deliberately and for the first time established a Christian state.[14] The Catholic Faith was to be the fundamental law of the state, and the fundamental principle of all the codes [15] the unity of the Catholic nation.

---

[13] Ureña y Smenjaud, p. 324.

[14] For estimates among the historians of the Council, see Ambrosio de Morales, *Crónica general de España,* lib. xii, c. 3; Mariana, *Hist. gen. de España,* lib. v, c. 15; P. Flores, *España* Sagrada, V, trat. 5, c. 2, VI, trat. 6, c. 4; M. de la Fuente, *Hist. Gen.,* lib. iv, c. 3; V. de la Fuente, *Hist. Eccles. de España;* D. José Amador de los Rios, *Hist. crit. de la Lit. de España;* Menéndez y Pelayo, *Hist. de los Heteredoxes españoles,* lib. i.

[15] Forum Iudiciorum, Primus Titulus, 1, 2; lib. xii, tit. ii, 1. 2-17; *Fuero Real,* lib. i, tit. i, 1; lib. iv. tit. i, 1, 2; *Ordenamiento Real de Castilla,* lib. i, tit. i, 1. 1; lib. viii, tit. v, 1. 1, tit. viii, 1. 3; *Las Siete Partidas, Partida Primera,* tit. i, *leyes* 1, 4, 6, 10, 11, *Partida Tercera,* tit. iii, *Partida Septima,* tit. xxvi, leyes 2, 4, 5, 6; *Nueva Recopilación* reproduces the laws of the *Ordenamiento Real,* as does also the *Novissima Recopilación.* All these references are from the texts as in *Los Códigos Españoles,* Madrid, 1847-51.

THE LEX VISIGOTHORUM

The link that bound all the peoples of the Iberian peninsula together was their common Catholic Faith. They saw all their problems in the light of its teaching, they never attempted a solution without first consulting its principles. They were Catholic first and Spanish second, that is, Spanish in the national sense; for as describing the people Spanish and Catholic were henceforth synonymous. Nationality in the modern sense was unknown to that age. The ecclesia Catolica explained satisfactorily anything that could be implied in the concept of civil society or the state. Their common Christianitas was a sufficient bond of union; without it, if they could have imagined such a contingency, their state would have perished.

Catholic principles had been introduced by way of the Theodosian code, but the spectacular acceptance of the Catholic Faith at Toledo so impressed the imagination of the people, that nothing in all their long and checkered history has been able to eradicate from their consciousness that their state is a Catholic state, based upon and ruled by Catholic principles. The most striking example of this is the fact that never in the colonies, when once the political link with Spain was broken, were the most anti-Catholic and freethinking elements ever able to remove from their constitutions the clauses declaring the Catholic religion to be the religion of the state and the practice of no other faith to be tolerated, without prolonged and bitter struggles. And in those countries where this clause was eliminated, political peace, justice and true prosperity departed with it.

Religious unity being the outward sign of the homogeneity and inner unity of their political being, the Spanish were always uneasy in the presence of alien peoples and alien cultures, unless these could be made to conform with their ideals.

The Third Council of Toledo was also important as having the public sanction of the king and for the legislation in regard to the Jews of Canon xiv. This restored the enactment of the *Breviario* of Alaric which had been abolished by Leovigild and may be seen in Book XII, *tít.* II *ley* 12 of the Liber Iudiciorum. *Leyes* 13, 14 and 16 of the same title were amplified by Sisebut and by Sisenandus from the Fourth Council of Toledo (canons 57-66). Chindaswinth, Recceswinth, Ervigio and Egica also made additions. Chintila developed legislation concerning the liberties of the Church. Chindaswinth was also very active.[16] So numerous were his laws that he may almost be regarded as initiating a new code, which was carried to completion by his son and successor Recceswinth (649-77). In many of these laws, Chindaswinth modified more or less profoundly different capitula in the Lex Antiqua and in the old Gothic laws, carrying out the general principles of transforming the code from personal law to territorial law, begun by Leovigild. Roman law, despite its formal rejection,[17] continued to influence legislation. Important sections of central Spain, under the power of the Byzantine Emperors from the reign of Athanagild (551), were conquered by Sisebut (624). In these territories the laws of Justinian were in force, having superseded the *Breviario* while the reformed code of Leovigild had not yet been put in force here. These Justinian laws thus continued to have force until the publication of the code of Recceswinth and were the laws to which he had reference in the clauses: De remotis alienarum gentium legibus and nolumus sive Romanis legibus seu alienis institutionibus amodo amplius convexari.

Until the publications of Carl Zeumer's researches Chin-

---

[16] For a list of his laws, see Ureña y Smenjaud, pp. 437-9.
[17] F. I., *Lib.* II, *tit.* I, *ley* 1, from Euric.

daswinth was considered the Justinian of Spain and the author of the code of Recceswinth, known formally as the Liber Iudiciorum, the Liber or the Forum Iudicum, but it is now established that the jurists of Recceswinth compiled this version of the Gothic-Spanish law. They did not aim to fuse the Lex Antiqua of Leovigild and the various Novellae and royal constitutions, which were the complement of this into a single code. They maintained the distinct characteristics of each of the varied elements, arranging them in order in books, titles or *eras*, *capitulos* or laws so that the Liber Iudiciorum is a compilation.[18]

Book I, De Instrumentis legalibus, based on the Etymologies of Isidore, constitutes an introduction to political philosophy relative to the legislator and the law.[19] The code does not really begin until Book II, the first law of which commences In Nomine Domini. This book takes up the applications and effects of laws, treats of the tribunals and judicial procedure. Book III develops principles of justice (*derecho*) in regard to matrimony, Book IV treats of the rights of the family and succession, Book V of contracts, Book VI of criminals and torture, Book VII of thefts and fraud, penal legislation, Book VIII of rural economics, Book IX of fugitives and deserters, asylums, immunities of temples, Book X of the division of the land, slaves, prescription in regard to property, Book XI of doctors, graves, merchants, fragments from the Lex Antiqua, Book XII of heretics and Jews.

From this it may be seen that the Liber Iudiciorum is a code devised exclusively for the use of the tribunals of justice. The public law of the Visigothic state controls when juridical relations are being determined and when the

[18] Ureña y Smenjaud, p. 447.

[19] Edition of Zeumer. The Academy edition of 1815 begins with the De Electione Principum.

exigencies of practical judgment demand it.[20] To the jurists of Recceswinth belong the greater part of the rubrics found at the beginning of each of the capitula though the Codex revisus of Leovigild may have contained some of them.[21] Recceswinth was also active in the Eighth, Ninth and Tenth Councils of Toledo and in various Novellae leges. Other laws were enacted by Wamba.

All this development towards a single code but reflects the aim of establishing one territorial law for Spain instead of the Roman custom of leaving to each people their laws, and of eliminating the personal laws of the barbarians. Recceswinth did not wish any longer to be tormented with Roman laws and foreign institutions. Ervigio complained of the multiplicity of litigation, the variety of interpretations, the resistance to the fulfillment of the laws, the indecision and lack of firmness in the judgments of the tribunals.[22]

In the Twelfth Council of Toledo, Ervigio designated a committee of theologians and jurists to draw up a revision of a reformed Visigothic code which was completed by October, 681.[23] His jurists preserved the inscriptions of the laws even when they altered the texts.[24] Ervigio also was

[20] Ureña y Smenjaud, p. 450.

[21] Idem, pp. 462, 464.

[22] Appointing this first in order and in place of introduction, we issue this constitution for the removal of errors from the law, because as clearness in the law is excessively useful for the people, so also obscurity in the laws disturbs the order of equity. For while very many times the laws are drawn up in good order, they are wrapped in a cloud of words, so that they themselves promote antagonism to them, nor do they clearly prevent the controversies of the litigants, and thus when they should put an end to sophistries, they foster new snares of deception against themselves. Hence there arises a diversity of pleas and they are brought forth in the controversies of the litigants. From this also is born the indecision of the judges, so that they do not know how, by checking or restraining, to put an end to the argument, and therefore waverings and doubt are always shown (Pragma suum emendatis legibus adsignantes illud primum ordine, prefationis et loco premittimus, quia, sicut legum evidentia populorum est excessibus utilis, ita sanctionum, obscuritas turbat ordines equitatis. Nam plerumque dum quedam bene ordinata nebuloso verborum tractu consistunt, ipsa sibi repugnantium nutriunt, dum litigantium controversias lucide non excluduunt sicque ubi debuerunt finem ferre calumniis, ibi novos contra se pariunt laqueos captionis. Hinc ergo diversitas causarum exoritur hinc controversie litigantium generantur, hinc etiam hesitatio iudicum nascitur, ita ut in finiendis vel compescendis calumniis habere terminum nesciant, que utique nutantia semper adprobantur et dubia, F. I., II tit. I, lex 1 Ervigio, ed. Zeumer).

[23] A list of the laws amended by Ervigio may be found in Ureña y Smenjaud, p. 148, 150-52.

[24] Idem, p. 499.

active in the Thirteenth Council of Toledo (November, 683) in which he confirmed the revision of the code (canon 9) and decreed an amnesty to all who had taken part in the uprising under Paulus in the reign of Chindaswinth (canon 1) and procured the personal security of priests and officials accused of treason, ordaining that no one could be deprived of his charge without manifest and clear evidence of blame and that the witness without suffering any imprisonment or blame in his person or property should be brought before the assembly constituted as a tribunal of clergy, seniors and *gardingos* (in publica sacerdotum, seniorum atque gardingorum discussione deductus. Canon 2). Canon 4 provided for protection for the royal family. This was included by Egica in the Titulus De electione principum, cap. 16.

Egica, in his *tomo regio,* made April 25, and presented to the Sixteenth Council of Toledo held in May, 693, proposed a reform of the code, desiring that all the misleading elements in the canons and edicts of the laws which from the time of Chindaswinth to the time of Wamba, a too hasty compilation had introduced, should be corrected in the light of justice and truth.[25] This evidently did not mean the radical change that one would expect, for not more was added than the De electione principum [26] and some Novellae leges. No particular manuscript of the Egican legislation has come down to us, and the official reforms of Egica appear confused with the Vulgata in the manuscripts of this collection. We have sixteen Novellae leges of Egica.[27] The revisions of Egica were probably promulgated in 694.

[25] Cuncta vero quae in canonibus vel legum edictis depravatata consistunt aut ex superfluo vel indebito coniecta fore patescunt, accommodante serenitatis nostrae consensu, in meridiem lucidae veritatis reducite, illis procul dubio legum sententiis reservatis, quae ex tempore dive memoriae praecessoris nostri domini Chindasvinti regis usque ad tempus domini Wambanis principis ex ratione depromptae ad sinceram iustitiam vel negotiorum sufficientiam pertinere noscuntur.

[26] Ureña y Smenjaud, p. 528.

[27] Idem, p. 507, pp. 531-34.

Confusion exists in regard to the form known as the Vulgata, some supposing it was the work of jurists of the eighth century, others that it originated at the end of the seventh century and contained the Novellae leges of Egica. The Vulgata, however, seems to be a collection of laws and commentaries existing from the Eurican legislation and it has accompanied all the official recasting of the lex Visigothorum, sometimes placed in appendices, sometimes as interpellations, to complete the existing codes.[28]

Such is a brief sketch of the origins of the famous Liber Iudiciorum. It was put into Spanish by order of Don Ferdinand III on April 4, 1241, as the *Liber de los Jueces*, and there are some variations between this version and the Latin texts. It was preserved in the Asturias during the invasion of the Arabs, and from here went to Castile and León; preserved in Sobrarve, it went from there to Cataluña, Aragon and Navarre. Zurita testifies to the fact of its being in force over this region, though in the latter territory it was augmented by the *Usatges* of mixed French origin taken over from the empire of Charlemagne. Throughout all Spain it was a species of common law and the background of all other legislation whether *fueros, behetrías* or of that for the cities of the *realengos.*[29]

Don Ferdinand III in his confirmation of the *fuero* for Toledo and also in that of the city of Córdova a little later follows this code. As he said in 1241, "I thus grant to you that all your judgments be made according to the Liber Iudicum, in the presence of ten of the most noble and wise among you who shall sit always with the *alcaldes* of the city for the examining of the judgments of the people, so that all may

[28] Ureña y Smenjaud, pp. 541-7.

[29] For a bibliography discussing the authority in which the Forum Iudiciorum and the old Visigothic laws and customs were held from the beginning of the Reconquest to the thirteenth century, consult Ballesteros, vol. II, pp. 569, 610, 693. Gama Barros and Marichalar y Manrique in particular give many examples.

follow in the testimonies in all the land of my dominion." And again "Likewise I decree and order that the Liber Iudicum which I sent to Córdova should be translated into the Spanish; and it shall be called the *Fuero* of Córdova with all that has been said above, and it shall be held by all forever as the *fuero*, nor shall any one dare to call it otherwise than the *Fuero* of Córdova. I order and command that every disturber and criminals in the estates within the bounds of Córdova which I shall bestow upon the archbishops, bishops, overseers, rich men, soldiers and clerics, shall come to trial according to the *Fuero* of Córdova."

In the course of a dispute in the time of his son, Don Alfonso X, in Talavera as to whether a certain case should be decided by the laws of the Forum Iudiciorum or the laws of the *Fuero de Castilla*, the king decided in favor of the former (1254). This was confirmed by Don Sancho in 1282, 1290 and in the *Cortes* of Valladolid in 1293, and the Forum Iudiciorum remained supreme to the end of this century. The *Ordenamiento* of Alcalá, dictated by Don Alfonso XI, recognized its authority. It was considered to have higher weight than the *Las Siete Partidas*. In the Laws of Toro the Catholic Kings confirmed the *Ordenamiento de Alcalá* which was inserted in the *Recopilación* of Don Philip II. In a *cédula* [30] of Don Charles III, July 15, 1778, it was once more confirmed,[31] and it has never been set aside.

This is not to say, however, that with the revival of the study of the Justinian texts in the thirteenth century, the interpretations of its principles did not vary. But before taking up the changes introduced by this, some analysis of the Forum Iudiciorum is necessary.

[30] *Cédula*, from the Latin schedula, diminutive of sheda, a sheet of paper. The *cédula real* was the warrant which the King, or the Council in his name, sent out in order to promulgate a law or decree of a general character, granting some favor or reward. As a form of publishing law, it did not differ from *pragmáticas sanciones* which were the decrees of the king in answer to petitions of the *Cortes*.

[31] *Los Códigos Españoles*, Vol. I, p. xlvii.

Chapter III

Principles of the Forum Iudiciorum, *Costumbres* of Tortosa and the *Usatges* of Barcelona

THE most significant part of the Forum Iudiciorum is the Primus Titulus, De electione principum. At the end of the title is a little homily,[1] justifying the Gothic kings in their codes and stating the principles which motivated their actions. Judgment, it says, is of two kinds, the first that of the Gospels, in which lies mercy enshrined and hidden the justice called talion. The second, that of the kingdom, which is manifest in the progress of the people and the maintenance of the cities.[2] It was not the intention of the Gothic kings to put down their judgments with such great cruelty as to reduce all to servitude, but there was such evil abroad, that if it were not dealt with, there would have been no peace or safety for the wise. Consequently the code was drawn up to cover the case of prevailing evils so that all could recognize the judgments of a Catholic king and of Christianity, and the code was to be binding upon all. In referring to the arrangement, the jurist goes on to say, that though the *ley antiqua* (Roman law) is taken advantage of, it becomes the *ley emendada.* For although it is necessary to have the law clear and precise so as to arrive at the truth, and the ancient Roman laws sought to end all doubt and discussion, it must be noted that these same engender con-

[1] *Los Códigos Españoles,* vol. I, pp. 103-4.
[2] Cf. Isidore of Seville, Lib. Sent., III, cap. xlviii, cap. xlix, 3.

tradictions and misery and throw all into perturbation, so much so that the argument of neither side can be disentangled, nor the reason of the litigants set forth, nor the struggle be ended, but arguments are multiplied, perfidy is strengthened and discord cometh without end.

In other words, codes are necessary to establish justice, to set forth the principles upon which judgments are to be made, and thus to bring about that peace so vital to the welfare of society. These principles are to be based upon the Catholic teaching which has for its aim the regulation of human relations and which lead to true concord, and not on the principles of the Roman law which so often give rise to wrangles over mere words.

The functions of the king in this scheme are shown forth in clauses one to eighteen of the Titulus Primus. The first principle is this: the king is given the name of king because he rules (as the priest is so called from the offering up of sacrifice), and ruling, he must rule piously, in the spirit of mercy, doing no injustice, or he shall lose the name of king. From which the ancients have the proverb: King you will be, if you will do right, and if you do not do right, you will not be king.[3] Thus the twin virtues which distinguish a king are truth and justice, for justice through him is truth.[4]

Secondly the king holds his title pursuant to the regard he has for the oath, taken before he receives his kingdom, to guard the law in all things. The king, further, should be elected in a council of bishops, the rich men of the court or

[3] Reges a recte agendo vocati sunt, ideoque recte faciendo regis nomen tenetur, peccando amittitur. Isidore of Seville, Lib. Sent., III, c. xlviii, 7; Etymologies, ix, c. 3 in Migne. Vol. 82. See also Horace, Epistulae, Lib. I, 1, lines 59-60, . . . At pueri ludentes, Rex eris, aiunt, si recte facies.

[4] In Latin text title I, 1, in Spanish text, II. This clause is not found in all the codices. Cf. also *Las Siete Partidas, Segunda Partida,* I, *título,* I, *ley* 6; Rex dicitur quasi rector a regendo, though it goes on to add kings rule not only in temporalities, but also in spiritualities. Cf. also in this same section, on rule (imperium), the King is the vicar of God in temporalities, as the Pope is in spiritualities, and the King is to defend the Faith. These laws are a curious instance of the crossing of the Roman law (Justinian) and the Catholic tradition. See also the Fourth Council of Toledo.

of the people, not in the forum of the city, nor in a council of the few, nor in a council of the *villanos* of the people.[5] The monarchy was not hereditary in the Visigothic Spanish kingdom.[6] The kings were to be of the Christian Faith, should rule justly and not for themselves alone.[7] The character of the one who should be king was also outlined. He should be a man of good customs and good lineage.[8]

The third principle brought out in this De electione principum, is that the authority of the king was to be respected and safeguarded by all, under pain of excommunication. It was against reason for any one to wish to gain the kingdom while the king still lived, and for this end to wish the death of the king, since to God alone belongs the knowledge of the hour of death.[9] Excommunication was the due of those plotting to get rid of the king, and the clergy were charged with the duty of informing the king of such actions, if knowledge of these should come to them.[10] The people also were bound to support the king, by virtue of their swearing allegiance, for there is nothing more displeasing to God than to say one thing with the mouth and mean another in the heart and mind. Excommunication was

[5] In the Latin text, non forinsecus aut conspiritatione pravorum aut rusticorum plebium seditioso tumultu (not irregularly, or in a conspiracy of the perverse, or in a seditious uprising of the country people). All references are to the seventh edition of the Liber Iudiciorum in the Spanish Academy edition published in *Los Códigos Españoles*. The Liber Iudiciorum is in Vol. I, the *Las Siete Partidas* in Vols. II, III and IV. Cf. also the Fourth and Eighth Councils of Toledo.

[6] Among the Novellae leges, constitutiones extravagantes, etc., placed by the authors of the Vulgata, appears a capitulo entitled, De Successione Rege, and it is attached to the De electione principum on the two codices Matritenses 772 and 12924. It represents the transformation of the Visigothic political principles into those of the new Christian states springing up during the Reconquest. It dates, according to Ureña y Smenjaud probably from the VIII-X centuries or more likely was written during the turbulent reign of Doña Urraca (1109-25), or what is less likely, at the end of the thirteenth century during the disputes between Don Sancho and the Infantes de la Cerda. The anonymous author of the Cod. Matrit. 772 says "vix ex multis manuscriptis libris, quos versavimus, in uno aut altero reperisse sine concilij conventus ve ullius, sine regis sine ullius auctoritas praescriptione." (Though he had consulted many manuscript books in none could he find any indication of a council or king which authorized it.) Urena y Smenjaud, pp. 548-49 for Latin text of this *capitulo*.

[7] De electione principum, Tit. IV. Cf. also the Fifth Council of Toledo.

[8] Ibid., Tit. V. Tit. VIII added neither religious, or slave, or foreigner, nor one not of the Gothic lineage. See also Fourth and Fifth Councils of Toledo.

[9] Tit. VI, and Fourth and Fifth Councils of Toledo.

[10] Tit. VII.

declared against all those who took up arms against the king, or who plotted to oppose him by force, and the bishops were to warn the clergy and the people that this law must be enforced.[11]

It is interesting to note that the clergy or *legos* taking part in an election of a king during the lifetime of the lawful king, or lending aid to a foreigner, whether bishop or ordained cleric, was also to be excommunicated, and the prince was not to spare such, and if he did he should be condemned before God. And it was the duty of the people to avenge the prince in such circumstances, also under pain of excommunication.[12] Title XI considers the breaking of the oath of allegiance to the king treason against the king and provided the sanction of excommunication.[13]

These ideas are reflected in *Las Siete Partidas,* which takes up the question of treason exhaustively, as befits the Roman lawyers. It considers treason as one of the greatest evils, a kind of leprosy in the body politic, and therefore those committing it should be separated from the others as lepers are.[14]

Attention is called to the fact that the point made in the matter of the relations between the prince and the people, is that the prince, or king, having taken an oath to be faithful to the laws of the people and holding his position on condition that he fulfill justice, and that the people on their part, having accepted him and given their oath of allegiance, both are bound to accept the resulting status. A violation of it is an offense meriting excommunication—a kind of death in life since it separated the one subject to its decree from

---

[11] Tit. IX. See also canon lxxv of the Fourth Council of Toledo. The penalty of excommunication is mentioned three times in this title.

[12] Titles X and XII.

[13] Title XI. See also *Lib.* II, *Tit.* I, *ley* vi; *Fuero Real, Lib.* I, *Tit.* II, *Lib.* IV, *Tit.* xxi, *leyes* 13, 25; *Ordenamiento de Alcalà, Tit.* xxxii, *leyes* 3, 4, 5.

[14] *Las Siete Partidas, Partida septima, Tit.,* II.

all those relationships which made life possible and fruitful here and hereafter—because the offense is not political but religious, since it is a violation of truth, of justice, of those ends for which God instituted authority and government. The contractual relations and obligations brought out by the mutual oaths of king and people were not merely between them alone, but also between them and God, not just because God was called to witness the truth of their oath, though of course that was an element important to a Catholic people, and thereby truth would be dishonored, but also because in taking these oaths, relationships were being established to maintain the relations of all to God based upon justice itself.

Now in the *Las Siete Partidas* this philosophical conception though not lost sight of, tends to become confused with the view of the sovereign as *in himself* requiring all support and obedience from the people. This idea derived from those who studied the Justinian code, who did not quite realize where they were going, while succeeding legists and sovereigns fell easily in line with this for various motives. From this date all the abuses of *lèse majesté* so fondly scored by democrats of later days.

Titles XIV, XV, XVI, and XVII of the De electione principum outline the safeguards which should also be extended to the family of the king.[15] Title XVIII protected the rights of the people. All those faithfully serving the king, should not lose any rights, dignities or possessions since to take them away is against reason and against right.[16]

The philosophy of law may be found in the two titles of Book I, entitled De Legislatore and De Lege. This section is really part of the De electione principum as explained

[15] See the Sixth Council of Toledo, also *Las Siete Partidas, Partida Segunda, Tit.* xv; *Partida Septima, Tit.* ii, *ley* 1; *Fuero Real, Tit.* iii.
[16] See also *Las Siete Partidas, Partida Segunda, Tit.* xxvii, *ley* 4; *Partida Tercera, Tit.* xviii, *ley* 51.

above, though placed at the beginning of the code in so many editions. It is taken over almost bodily from Book V of the Etymologies of Isidore (and also Book II). Isidore took the theories of the Roman law as he found them in the text books of Gaius and Ulpian, in the Theodosian code and the Sentences of Paulus, but supplemented them by the principles developed by the Catholic writers up to his time, particularly St. Augustine, and worked them over into a clear coherent system. He makes the distinction between Divine and human law, and is insistent upon the idea that law arises out of custom, lex being but the written ordinance.[17] Law is in accordance with reason, and anything in accordance with reason, provided it agrees with religion, is in harmony with knowledge, and is beneficial to salvation. Law is not then something "passed" or made by some one, it is but the expression of reason, but reason that must take into consideration the facts and needs of salvation. It is the enactment of the people [18] and either permits something, forbids something or punishes.[19] It is necessary to bridle the powers of harm, to keep innocence safe among the wicked.[20] And he sums up his principles in the famous criterion: Law must be just, *honesta* [21] possible, according to nature and custom, necessary, useful, clear, for the advantage of all.[22]

The two titles of Book I of the Liber Iudiciorum reflect these principles in the discussion of the nature of law. Title I lays down the principles for the legislator. In the first place law-making is an art. It is an art to be learned, and

[17] Etymol., Bk. V, c. ii, 1; c. iii, 2 in Migne, Vol. 82.
[18] Etymol., Bk. V, c. x; see also Bk. II, c. x, 4.
[19] Etymol., Bk. V, c. xix, see also Bk. ii, c. x, 4.
[20] Etymol., Bk. V, c. xx.
[21] The Christian connotation of the Roman honestus amplified the meaning of worthy, fitting, due, into something morally perfective of human nature.
[22] Etymol. Bk. V, c. xxiv; see also Bk. II, c. x, 6.

once acquired, it is of value only if it is practised for truth, not through conformity, nor for the subtlety of syllogisms, nor for disputation but for good and honest principles *(comendamientos*, possibly *comezamientoz?)*.[23] Law is to be framed not through disputing, but by justice,[24] according to possibilities and for the common good,[25] and by a legislator who looks to God and to truth and who knows how to speak openly, clearly and without difficulty of being understood.[26]

In the second place, the legislator needs certain characteristics; he should be intelligent in judging right, resolute, circumspect; at times he should pardon, he should punish the one who doth ill, but use temperance in giving the punishment; he should not show more justice towards one man than towards another.[27] And he should serve all.[28]

---

[23] *Ley* 1. See also *Fuero Real, Lib.* 1, *Tit.* vi; *Las Siete Partidas, Partida Primera, Tit.* I, especially *ley* 8: Lex debet esse perfecta et facta super his, quae possunt occurrere secundum communem naturam bonisque vocabulis et inteligibilibus et plane composita, nec debent leges ad invicem contrariari, and *ley* 13: Intellegi lex debet bene et recte in saniori meliori sensu, secundum eius verba nec debet per abbreviaturas scribi. (Law should be fashioned and made upon these principles,—what is possible according to common nature, and it should be composed openly and in good intelligible words, nor should laws be mutually contradictory. A law should be comprehensible fully and rightly in the best sense, according to its words, nor should it be written in abbreviations).

[24] *Ley* 2. See also *Fuero Real, Lib.* I, *Tit.* vi, *ley* 1, where it is added "and speaking much, as they do in the halls of the philosophers."

[25] *Ley* 3. See also *Las Siete Partidas, Partida Primera, Tit.* x, *ley* 11: Legis conditor debet amare Deum et in ea condenda prae oculis eum habere, ut sic perfecta et iusta. Item debet iustitiam et bonam commune diligere et scire bonum ab illicito separare, nec pudeat eum si iniusta sibi videatur corrigere. (The lawmaker should love God and in establishing the law should have Him before his eyes, so that it may be perfect and just. Likewise he should value justice and the common good and should know how to separate the good from the unlawful, nor should it shame him if he seems to correct the unjust in himself).

[26] *Leyes* 4, 5, 6. See also *Las Siete Partidas, Partida Segunda, Tit.* IV, *leyes*, 1, 2, 3. *Ley* 1: Vox seu verbum est eorum quae sunt in animo manifestatio et est magna sermonis utilitas verba prius ad liman veniant quam ad linguam quia semel emissum volat irrevocable verbum; *Partida Primera, Tit.* I, *leyes* 8, 9, 11. (The word is the manifestation of those things which are in the mind and it is of great utility for speech, if the word should first be corrected before it reaches the tongue, because a word once released is irrevocable.)

[27] *Ley* 7. See also *Las Siete Partidas, Partida Tercera, Tit.* V, *ley* xli. The *Partida Tercera* gives us a discussion of justice in the concrete and the abstract. In the prologue to this *Partida*, is laid down the general principle that Our Lord made all things very completely, by His great wisdom disposing each one in his state, and in this way He shows what is His great goodness and justice, and in what manner those should maintain it who have to do justice on earth. They require three things: first they should have the will to desire and to love justice (reflecting the Book of Wisdom, c. I., V. I.); second they should know how to do justice, and third, how to maintain it against those who would oppose it. Consequently judges should administer justice strictly in conformity with the laws and without confusing mercy and rigor.

In *Titulo* I, justice, because the best, is one of the things to be most strictly maintained in the world. It is the fountain whence flows all right; not only has justice

Title II, De lege, lays down the principle that law is a thing of reason.[29] The end of law is to show forth to the people the right way of living and to be the mistress of virtues.[30] Law should be simple, clear, manifest to all [31] and binding on all.[32]

The third principle set forth in this title, is that through justice the citizen is defended and in the peace and true concord of the citizens, all enemies are overcome.[33] Since all things should be fulfilled with a view to peace, and all struggle should cease among princes and among the citizens and among the people and within families, the people aided by the laws and armed with justice will do better than armed with weapons.

The next most famous codes, of this period after the Forum Iudiciorum are the *Costumbres* of Tortosa, the *Fuero*

---

to be maintained in all litigation but also in regard to all the other things that concern men, what they wish to do by act or say by mouth.

Lex 1: Justitia est virtus radicata et perpetua durans in iustorum voluntate, ius suum unicuique tribuens: haec assimilatur fonti perenni (Justice is the root and eternal virtue enduring in the will of the just, attributing to each one his due; it is compared to a perennial fountain).

Lex 2: Per iustitiam vivunt homines recte et mensurate et absque errore; et eius praemio boni meliores, eiusque formidine mali boni efficiuntur; hac mundus sustentatur, et hominis reddit pacificos: amanda est velut pater ac mater; reveranda et obedienda velut bonus dominus, servanda ut vita (Through justice men live rightly and accurately, and removed from error, and as a reward of it the good are better, and in the fear of it evils are made into good; it sustains the world and restores peace to men; it is loving as a father and a mother, it is reverenced and obeyed as a good master, it is guarded as life).

Lex 3: Iuris praecepta sunt honeste vivere alterum non laedere ius suum unicuique tribuere (The precepts of justice are to live as is fitting, not to injure another, but to attribute to each his due).

In this code we have the approach to a fusion of the ideas on justice of the Graeco-Roman philosophy with the Christian interpretation that justice here on earth is the reflection of that Divine Justice established by God, and that it is because of this reflection that the obligation to seek and fulfill justice binds. This is the Augustinian philosophy, not the Stoic (for a brief comparison of the two philosophies in regard to law see article by Rev Moorhouse I. X. Millar, S.J. in, "Thought" for March, 1928, "The Origin of Sound Democratic Principles in Catholic Tradition"). The Forum Iudiciorum has this idea, but the later code elaborates it and brings out the shadings as befits the more civilized times in which it was drawn up.

[28] *Leyes* 8, 9. Cf. also *Las Siete Partidas, Partida Segunda, Tít.* X, *ley* 2.

[29] *Ley* 1 repeats the idea that laws should not be made through sophisms, but by force of justice. The law is not to be made in argument but by reason, since bad customs are not to be restrained by beautiful words but by virtues.

[30] *Leyes* 2, 5.

[31] *Ley* 5.

[32] *Ley* 3: The law governs the city and governs all in all of life, and thus it is given to men as to women, to great as to small, to the wise and to the not-wise, to the noble and to the vulgar, and that which is given above all the other things for the prince and for the people, and shines as the sun in defending all.

[33] *Ley* 6.

of Jaca of Aragon [34] and the Usatici or *Usatges* of Barcelona. Other important codes are the Constitutions of Cataluña [35] and the *Constituciones de la Generalidad de Cataluña.*[36]

The *Costumbres* of Tortosa

In the *Libre de les costums generales scrites de la insignes ciutat de Tortosa*, the institutions of the Catalan people may be studied with advantage. Oliver y Esteller considers it a more interesting study than the *Usatges* of Barcelona as it covers all phases of law. Tortosa (civitas Dertossae of the Romans, Tortoxa of the Arabs) dates from the reign of Augustus, though an earlier Iberian town was on the same site. A metropolitan city under Roman rule, it kept this status under the Arabs and Christian princes and was made a marquisate under Aragonese rule.[37]

The Catalan term *costuma* (plural *costums*) is derived from *coutume*, used in the north and center of France and in Portugal to designate statutes or particular laws of a single town (*población*) or sometimes of a territory. The codes or compilations use indifferently *coutumes* (as *Coutumes* of Aigues Mortes, or *fór, fórs, furs, forum* as *fórs* of Béarn). La Ferrière in his *Histoire du Droit français*, says *coutumes* is taken from the ancient language *euskaro*, but Du Cange prefers to trace it to the Latin consuetudo. The Spanish word *costumbre* however has not the exact, concrete, juridical sense of consuetudo, but in the Middle

---

[34] The *Fuero de Jaca*, granted to the town in 1064 and confirmed by Don Sancho Ramirez, was reproduced from an earlier one granted by Count Galindo Aznárez. Muñoz y Romero hold that customary right (*derecho*) existed in Jaca which explains the saying of Don Alfonso II that Castile and Aragon went to Jaca to learn its usages and customs.

[35] *Constitucións y altres drets de Catalunya*, Barcelona, 1588.

[36] These are the glosses or interpretations of the *Usatges*, according to the jurist, Oliva, and written by Pedro Albert, Canon of Barcelona. Mieres, T., Apocatus super constituionibus curiorum generalium catalonia, Barcelona, 1621. For a bibliography on these and of some recent editions of the *Usatges*, consult Ballesteros, II, p. 692.

[37] Oliver y Esteller, B., *Historia del derecho en Cataluña Mallorca y Valencia y el Código de la Costumbres de Tortosa*, Madrid, 1876-, Vol. I: p. 245, *Carta de población.*

Ages consuetudo was used as the equivalent for a law preserved or transmitted by custom. Others hold *costums* is the written *usos* (mores, *moeurs*), while *usos* means traditions. Others interpret *costums* to be *usos* approved by the sovereign power, and consuetudo or *coutume* or *fuero* to refer to the Laws of the Visigoths.[38] According to contemporary documents and the official language of the Middle Ages, *costuma, coutume,* consuetudo, *usatges, usaiges, usatici, libertades, franquesas, franchises* were frequently used synonymously.[39]

The *Costumbres* of Tortosa seem to have been first promulgated in 1279 (certainly before 1294), and edited probably in 1272. The original which had been preserved in the archives of Tortosa, was destroyed by revolutionaries in 1854, only a few sheets being rescued from the fire. The edition of 1539 by the jurist, Juan Amich, is considered an exact copy.[40] It was in force until the reign of Don Philip V, was restored by the *Cortes* of 1812 and is still influential.[41] Many Catalan jurists had studied at the law schools of Montpellier and Toulouse and the *Costumbres* show the Roman influence in form and arrangement somewhat in the manner of the *Las Siete Partidas* [42] though the *Partidas* are more elegant. From Montpellier and Toulouse, the influence of the Justinian code spread through southern France and the Spanish march. It appears in the written though not in the customary law, and is derived not from the texts of the Digest, but from the interpretations of Placentius, Baldus

---

[38] Cf. discussion on origin of the word *fuero* in *Las Siete Partidas, Primera Partida, Tit.* II, prologue, and pages 66-7 of this essay.

[39] Oliver y Esteller, I, pp. 119-24.

[40] Idem, I, pp. 135-38. The text according to this edition is published in Catalan in Vol. IV.

[41] Idem, I, pp. 169-75.

[42] Oliver y Esteller rather complains that the Castilian code was "the utopia of a crowned philosopher," while the Catalans and Valencians reveal a more practical and positive spirit (I, pp. 218-9). For an interesting comparison between the two see, I, pp. 386-90. For the maritime customs of Tortosa and comparison of them with the *Libro del consulado de mar*, see III, app. 631.

and Azo. These were not popular. The *Costumbres* were drawn up to reform conditions in Tortosa, as the introduction says.[43] It is especially valuable as a study of the organization of society and the regulation of the relations between Jew, Christian and Mussulman.

To sum up its principles: in the social order, the guarantees of the right of man to express himself freely in the arts and sciences were laid down, the inviolability of person and domicile were recognized, and equality in the administration of the collective interests was admitted. In the political order, the *Costumbres* might be said to have fused feudalism with the status of the *municipio* on the principles of justice, authority and liberty as held by St. Thomas Aquinas.[44] The rulers were elected by the people.

The chief influences on the development of the *Costumbres* derive from the customs of Provence, by way of the Arlés codes,[45] the *Condado* of Bigorre (giving the Basque, the Ibero-Latin and the Ibero-Gothic traditions), Perpignan, the *Usatges* of Barcelona, the Visigothic laws, the Theodosian code and the Canon law. The influence of the *Usatges* was slight as in many places there was great repugnance to consider it as common law.[46]

The *Usatges* of Barcelona

The origins of the political history of Navarre and Aragon are very obscurely known.[47] It is certain, however, that the

[43] *Aprouasen aquelles costumes quels parrien bones: e reprouassen aquelles que contenrıen peccat et embargarien justicia* (To approve those customs which appear good and to reform those which induce to sin, i. e. if they ran counter to Divine, natural or positive law, and to enforce justice), Oliver y Esteller, I, p. xxii and pp. 129-30.

[44] Oliver y Esteller, I, pp. 375-81. *Libre de les Costums*, Lib. IX, c. iii, *Rúbrica* De verborum significatione : Jus est ars boni et equi cuius merito justum ab injusto, equuŭn ab iniquo, licitum ab illicito, separamus, unicuique quid suum est dando (Ius is the art of the good and just, by the merit of which, we separate the just from the unjust, equity from evil, the lawful from the unlawful, by giving to each one what is his).

[45] Statuta sive leges municipales Arelatis, edited 1162-1202.

[46] Oliver y Esteller, I, pp. 276-8.

[47] de la Fuente, V., *Estudios críticos sobre la historia y el derecho de Aragón*, Madrid, 1885, II, p. 7. For a bibliography on this much disputed question, see Ballesteros, II, pp. 295-6.

Arabs never established their power in the fastnesses of the Pyrenees, and from this area the reconquest of the eastern kingdoms started. There existed two neighboring zones, one which was normally independent but sometimes felt the power of Mussulman arms; the other formed the *Frontera Superior*, ruled by Mohammedan governors. It was always more or less in rebellion, receiving aid both from the Basques of the Pyrenees and from the Franks. During the confusion of the Arab state at the end of the ninth century, the Kingdoms of Navarre and Aragon were able to constitute themselves. No hope was to be expected from the empire of Charlemagne, which had lost all prestige, and unless the natives organized their own resources, they would be lost. According to Ximénez de Embún,[48] after the link uniting Pamplona with the Franks had been broken, there arose, sometime in the second third of the ninth century, a chieftain, Iñigo Arista, who sought to establish Pamplona into an independent state. At the time Pamplona happened to be free from the power of the Arab chiefs (of the Beni-Muza family at Saragossa). From here he descended to the plains of Navarre, and by the strength of his prowess deserved the leadership of the natives. His son, García, succeeding him, married the royal Doña Urraca and put Navarre on a firm footing. A line of distinguished kings followed, noted either for their organizing ability or their success against the Moors. Navarre played a prominent part in the affairs of Castile and Aragon, until the time of Don Sancho García IV *el Noble*, who was assassinated in 1076, when the Navarrese elected Don Sancho Ramírez of Aragon their king.

While the Beni-Muza were contending for the possession of Córdova, a chief, Aznar, captured Jaca, and another

---

[48] *Ensayo histórico acerca de los origenes de Aragón y Navarra,* Saragossa, 1878.

chief, Ramón, made himself master of the property of Pallás, thus forming the nucleus of a little independent state adjoining the Spanish march. Aznar took the name of Count of Aragon from the most important river of this region and made alliances with the ruler of Pamplona. Through a series of marriages between the two families, both states were united under Don García Sánchez I of Pamplona. After the death of Don Sánchez Garcés III *el Mayor*, his son, Ramírez, received the little kingdom of Aragon. As Ramírez I he annexed Sobrarbe and Ribagorza. During the reign of his son, Navarre and Aragon were united (1076). It was this Don Sanchez Ramírez who confirmed the laws of Jaca. He was most active against the Moors and the same policy was followed by his sons Don Pedro and Don Alfonso I *el Batallador* who succeeded in taking Saragossa. After a glorious reign, during which the boundaries of Aragon were widely extended, he was succeeded by his brother Don Ramíro II, who had become a Benedictine monk. He lacked the character to hold his own against the encroachments of Castile and was content to be known as Lord of Aragon, Sobrarbe and Ribagorza. This did not suit Don García Ramírez of Navarre, and a treaty was arranged between them by which the two kingdoms were to be again reunited and Don Ramíro was to take the civil authority while Don García Ramírez commanded the armies. Later the latter plotted against his ally, who thereupon endeavored to secure the aid of Castile against Navarre. Meantime Don Ramíro had received the necessary dispensation from the Roman Pontiff and had married Iñez of Poitiers. When their daughter, Petronila, was born, a contest for the succession began and the Aragonese, disliking the thought of a Castilian marriage, succeeded in having arranged a marriage between

Petronila and Ramón Berenguer IV, Count of Barcelona (August 11, 1137) and thus the way was paved for the union of the two states.[49] This was not considered a simple dynastic change as the Aragonese were extremely jealous lest their laws and customs might become confounded with those of Barcelona.[50] This union brought into contact two different social organizations. The Ibero-Roman Aragon was agricultural while the more Gothic and feudal Cataluña was devoted to industry. The people here were naturally *entrepreneurs* and took to the pursuit of profits. Nevertheless the two peoples blended very well together, due chiefly to the prudent policy of Don Ramón and Doña Petronila, in granting *fueros* and building up *municipios* on the style of Italian republics, departing from the customs of the *Usatges.*

The *Condado* of Barcelona was the nucleus out of which developed eventually by the addition of surrounding territory the principality of Cataluña.[51] That territory, lying between the Pyrenees and the Mediterranean and bounded by the lands of the Aragonese on the west and Valencia on the south, in Roman times formed part of Tarraconense, then became the Spanish March (*Marca Hispaniae*) and finally Cataluña. The population was mixed, possibly a trace of Greek, an indigenous group around Pallás, Urgel, Cerdaña and Berga, a strong Roman element in Llobregat in the Pyrenees. This last, the March properly so called (name given by the French) was later known as Cataluña the old (in the twelfth century) and formed the *condados* of Gerona

[49] For documents on the union of Aragón and Cataluña, see *Colección de documentos inéditos del archivo general de la Corona de Aragón*, IV, *núm.* 24, 25, 26, 27, 28, 31; Zurita, *Anales de Aragón*, *lib.* viii, *c.* 18.

[50] Oliver y Esteller, B., *La nación y la realeza en los estados de la corona de Aragón*, discourse read before the Academy of History in Madrid, June 22, 1884, p. 18, relying on *Col. de Doc. inéd. Aragón*, IV, and appendices in Bofarull A. de, *La confederación catalana aragonesa*, Barcelona, 1872.

[51] For a bibliography on the origins of Cataluña, see Ballesteros, II, pp. 339-40.

and Barcelona.[52] The Moors occupied the region around Lérida and Tarragona, or Cataluña the new. The Goths and Franks left their influence more in the political institutions than in the blood of the people.

According to Codera,[53] the mountain regions of Cataluña remained free from the Arab power, though Gerona, Barcelona and Narbonne came under their sway. Charlemagne in 778 undertook the conquest of the Spanish march with the aid of independent Christian chiefs of the neighborhood and was able to put Franks in charge of Gerona. The Reconquest in this part of Spain was started under Frankish auspices, though possibly later the Christian Spanish might have succeeded without Frankish aid. The policy of Charlemagne in establishing strong ramparts for his own kingdom helped considerably. The privilege of Charlemagne of 812 testifies to the existence of the *condados* of Rousillon, Besalú and Barcelona. The document of 819 recording the consecration of the Church of Santa Maria de Seo of Urgel, mentions the *condados* of Pallars, Urgel and Cerdaña. The counts of Barcelona were dependent upon the French until the time of Wilfredo or Guifre I in 874. His successors took the title of Duke of Gotica or Marquis of Getas, and when it was definitely constituted a state in the twelfth century, of Gothalaunia. Though the *condado* once again fell under French control, it soon recovered independence and under Don Ramón Berenguer I reached the boundaries of the present territory of Cataluña.[54] This Count Ramón Berenguer and his wife, Doña Adalmodis, confirmed the *Usatges*.

[52] The word Cataluña, or in the Latin Catalonia or Catalaunia according to Balari, is derived from castellanus, the guard of the castle. In French this became *chastelain* and *châtelain* in the low Latin of the time, *castlanus, castlá, catlá, carlá,* and the people *Catalanes,* since there were so many castles in this region, whence Catalán and Cataluña, which name appears in 1194.

[53] *Estudios críticos de historia árabe española.*

[54] It was his descendant, Don Ramón Berenguer IV, who married Petronila of Aragon in 1137.

This code[55] was derived from an earlier code of the Emperor Lothair II and reflects the Romano-Gothic-Franco tradition from the Theodosian code. The original text is lost, but an attentive reading of a later recasting, made possibly during the reign of Don Ramón Berenguer IV or Don Alfonso II (second half of the twelfth century), reveals the primitive wordings. As Ballesteros notes, the present tense calls attention to the *usatge* as custom, and the subjunctive is used to express the mandate confirming it as law.[56] The word *usatge* was variously used as *derecho,* tithe, tax, tribute or custom. And hence, according to Balari y Jovany,[57] the *Usatges* is equivalent to a code of customs in the sense of practices followed so long that they had the force of law. *Usatges* were called usaticos terrae (1091), lex usuaria (twelfth century), mores curiae barchinonensis (1157), forum et consuetudinem cataloniae (1184).

It is not definitely known who first drew up the text of the *Usatges* of Barcelona, though since the researches of Balari, many conjectures have been made, pointing to Ponç Bofill March, who studied jurisprudence under his famous father, Ervigio March. Don Berenguer Ramón I, whose tutor he was according to Balari, named him judge of the palace. Between 1035-68 he lived in retirement and devoted himself to study. He was named a member of the Assembly in which the *Usatges* was confirmed as the one most competent,

---

[55] For an account of the texts of this, see *Córtes de los Antiguos reinos de Aragón y de Valecia y Principado de Cataluña,* Madrid, 1896, I, pp. 5-9. In this volume may be found also the Latin texts with the variants of the different manuscripts, pp. 10-45, and the Catalan text from a manuscript of the thirteenth century (Appendix I). The Cortes of 1413 ordered a compilation of the *Usatges* with the Acts of the Cortes and other laws of Cataluña, but it was not published until the time of Don Fernando II. By order of the Cortes this was revised and printed in 1588-9 in three volumes, and revised again by order of the Cortes of Barcelona in 1702, printed in 1704. The text of this edition appears in Appendix II. Appendices IV and V contain the list of printed editions and manuscripts. The edition of 1544 has a commentary by the jurists Jacobus and Guillermus Vallcsicca and Jacobus Calicuis. This text was published by Marichalar Y Manrique in Volume VII of the *Historia de la Legislación del derecho de España,* Madrid, 1861.

[56] Vol. II, pp. 693-4.

[57] Ibid., p. 694.

probably, to draw up the text.[58] The need for a code had long been felt. During the period of Frankish influence, the people lived under various capitularies, such as those of the Praeceptum pro Hispaniae of Charlemagne, the Constitutiones de Hispanis (815-44), and others, the greater number of which regulated property rights as was natural at a time when repopulation, settlement and defense were the great needs. Barcelona was made the capital in 801 and its governor or count had a special position [59] and functions corresponding to those of a feudal lord. He had the title of prince to emphasize his dignity as chief among the governors, but was more frequently called count, with territorial jurisdiction. According to Father Fita [60] the first *Cortes* of Barcelona was held in May, 1064 at Gerona in which Count Berenguer Ramón I and his wife Doña Adalmodis confirmed the *Usatges*, holding to the constitutions of peace and truce among Christians and those of the ecclesiastical *fueros* and the protection of the Jews granted under the disciplinary sanction of the Council over which the Papal Legate presided. It was held in the cathedral church and attended by the Bishops of Barcelona, Vich and Gerona, abbots, magnates and good men (*omes buenos*).[61] Father Fita considers

---

[58] Ballesteros, II, pp. 695-6.

[59] Idem, II, p. 635 sq.

[60] *Cortes de los Antiguos reinos de Aragón y de Valencia y Principado de Cataluña*, I, p. 5.

[61] The word boni homines (*omes buenos* in Spanish) used here and also in the Forum Iudiciorum (*Lib.* VI, *Tít.* I, *ley* 4) signified according to *Las Siete Partidas* (*Partida septima, Lib.* IV, *Tit.* xxx, *ley* 31) an ordinary judge of the court, continuing the tradition of Roman and Visigothic times (Pérez-Pujol, II, pp. 276-81; IV, pp. 174-76, 266). Another term for boni homines was probi homines. These had a place in the royal curia and according to Savigny (*Hist. du Droit romain*, I) were the citizens who had the exercise of full rights. The probi homines of the *Costumbres de Tortosa*, were the successors of the aristocratic class (honorati) of the Romano-Gothic cities, whose prerogatives in regard to justice were exercised by distinguished citizens during the Reconquest (Oliver y Esteller, I, p. 62; II, pp. 116-21).

Two hypotheses are current as to the meaning of probi homines, or *prohoms* as it is sometimes written. There were those who had sufficient property to support them without having to work. The Romano-Gothic tradition leans towards this view, according to which in order to enter the Curia it was necessary to have some property. There is a distinction in the *Costumbres de Tortosa* and the *Usatges* between the free man who is a Christian and the one who has the dignity of citizen. The latter, as living on his income whether from capital or land, represented a more stable class in the community.

The second hypothesis is that the probi homines formed a kind of magistracy, a signi-

that the purely civil character of this assembly is not conclusively proved. Other authorities (de Pujades, Masdeu, Flórez, Capmany, Bofarull, Ballaguer, Balari and Ortiz de la Vega) deny this. Balari considers that Zurita has confused an assembly held by Don Ramón Berenguer I to promulgate the *Usatges* with the Council of Gerona, practically contemporaneous, over which the Papal Legate presided. At this assembly, according to Balari, three *vizcondes,* thirteen magnates (*comitores y valvasores*) and three judges assisted, only one an ecclesiastic, the canon and jurist, Ponç Bofill March.[62]

The tribunals relied on the authority of the Forum Iudiciorum as numerous documents in the archives of Barcelona, Urgel, Ampurias, Pallás, Cerdaña and Rosello testify.[63] In the *Usatges* it is expressly stated that the object was not to set aside the Gothic code but to supplement it on matters on which it was silent.[64] The Forum Iudiciorum was observed until the fifteenth century and quoted by the jurist, Jacobo de Maraquilles in his glosses on the *Usatges.*[65] The purpose of the code was to arrange the relations of the various social classes, those between vassals and lords, the

---

fication in use in southern Gaul and the Spanish march. Oliver y Esteller considers that the *Costumbres* is not clear on this point. According to the documents of these regions in the eleventh, twelfth and thirteenth centuries, the probi homines appear as the successors of the boni homines, who in turn succeeded the judices electi and ancient decuriones. They had a true public character in the municipal hierarchy, as they were citizens elected to govern the cities of the Roman tradition. It was not an honorific title, but a social distinction in an effective exercise of a public function. Hence Oliver y Esteller decides that the probi homines are the citizens who exercised administrative and judicial functions, and these took their seats in the curias as a body of men experienced and skilled in government.

[62] Ballesteros, II, p. 640-41.

[63] See the Placitum of 875 given by the Missus of the Governor of Gothia to decide a dispute between the Count of Rosella and the Bishop of Elna (Oliver y Esteller, I, p. 258). For authority in Narbonne see a constitution of Pope John VIII (878).

[64] *Cortes de los Antiguos reinos de Aragón y de Valencia y Principado de Cataluña,* I, pp. 10-11: Hoc enim fecit comes libri Iudiciorum auctoritate, que dicit: Sane adiciendi leges si justa novitas causarum exegerit principalis elecjio necessariam habet et potestate regis discrecione tractetur qualiter exoritum negocium inseratur (For the count does this by the authority of the Liber Iudiciorum, which says: Indeed it is necessary for a just justification for the introduction of a novelty in the laws to have the selection of the prince, and it may be undertaken by the authority and at the discretion of the king, in so far as the development of business requires its insertion).

[65] Commentaria Jacobi de Maraquilles super usaticis Barchinonae, Barcelona, 1505.

rule, regalias and rights of the prince, and to set punishment for the violations of truces and treaties. The influence of the Forum Iudiciorum is seen in the section on homicide and criminals [66] and the Constitutions Auctoritate et rogatu [67] and Princeps namque [68] in the obligation of the prince or king to uphold justice for his subjects, directly or indirectly through his officials,[69] and to heed the *greuges* or *gravias* (petitions of the *Cortes*), and in the principle that justice is the foundation of all society and without it the land and the people perish.[70] Law is held to be a species of right derived from custom, and the whole of the Constitution 146 is reminiscent of the fifth book of the Etymologies and the Forum Iudiciorum.[71]

Ballesteros does not hold that the *Usatges* are derived from custom, he says they were a spontaneous manifestation of the free will of the sovereign and an evidence of his power to legislate.[72] This is not quite correct. In a further

---

[66] Cf. Forum Iudiciorum, *Lib.* II, *Tit.* IV, *ley* 1; *Lib.* V, *Tit.* VII.

[67] Cf. Forum Iudiciorum, *Lib.* IV, *Tit.* V, *ley* 1; *Lib.* V, *Tit.* II, *ley* 6.

[68] Cf. Forum Iudiciorum, *Lib.* II, *Tit.* IV, *leyes* 8, 9.

[69] See Constitution 50: Omnes homines, tam milites quam rustici, iurent senioribus suis sicut ipsi iudicare fecerint iuste in placitis sive in iudiciis. Seniores, vero, hominibus suis nequaquam (All men, soldiers as well as the country people, shall swear to their lords just as they themselves may have done to judge justly in decisions or judgments. The lords also to their men, by all means).

[70] Quoniam per iniquum principem et sive veritate et sive iustitia periit omne tempore terra et habitatores eius. Constitution 65.

Quia fides et iustitia et pax et veritas principis quibus omne gubernat regnum et plusquam regnum valent (Because by the faith, justice, truth and peace of the prince, he governs all the kingdom, and the kingdom by this advances), Constitution 67.

Et quia terra sive iustiticia non potest vivere (and because a land without justice cannot survive), Constitution 90.

[71] Unaqueque gens propriam sibi ex consuetudine elegit legem. Longa enim consuetudo pro lege suscipitur. Lex autem iuris est species. Mos vero longa consuetudo, autem, est ius quoddam moribus institutum quod pro lege suscipitur. Nam quod rex et imperator edidit constitucio vel edictum vocatur, omne autem ius legibus et moribus constat; mos vero est vetustate probata consuetudo. Institucio equitatis duplex est, nunc in legibus nunc in moribus. Privilegia autem sunt leges privatorum quasi private leges. Nam privilegium inde dictum est quod in privato feratur (Also and of right, the people select the law for themselves from their custom. For, for a long time, custom has been taken for law. Law, moreover, is a kind of right. Custom is also use established for a long time. Moreover, it is a right in the same way instituted by usage, which is taken for law. For what the king or emperor command, is called a constitution or edict. All right (ius), however, stands rooted in law and custom, for custom is a usage, approved for a very long time. The establishment of equity has a dual foundation, in laws and in customs. Moreover privileges are laws of private persons (i.e., not officials), and serve as laws for such. Hence it has been said that a privilege is something which is carried out in private).

[72] Ballesteros, II, p. 640.

passage [73] he attempts on the authority of Balari to establish how from the authority inherent in the prince is deduced his power of legislating, executing and judging. In the *Usatge* 65 of the Code beginning Quoniam per iniquum principem, Ballesteros finds stated the principle that authority comes from God, as taught by St. Paul. Though this authority as a function of sovereignty, includes executive, legislative and judicial powers, it must be remembered that all these terms were interpreted in the light of the principles of the Forum Iudiciorum.[74] The legislative power of the prince was not to be exercised without the aid of and in consultation with, the good men of the kingdom,[75] and law was recognized as a species of right derived from custom, as shown above.

The *Usatges* took a form somewhat different to that of the Forum Iudiciorum because of the feudal influence present in Cataluña as a legacy from the French rule, and possibly because the early independent counts of Cataluña were of the Carolingian stock [76] and hence had the ideas of this family. The *Usatges* was the attempt to reconcile the practice of the old allodial system of property with the newer system of benefices and *honores* (tributes, taxes, rights) on the basis of the traditional principles as found in the Forum Iudiciorum, and as such was most certainly not intended to be the expression of the Roman law principle, the will of the prince has the force of law. This principle appears stated in Constitution 70,[77] but this reflects the crossing of

---

[73] Ibid., p. 642.

[74] See Chapter V, Part II, of this essay.

[75] Nos sepedichi principes Raimundus et Almodis, consilio et auxilio nostrorum nobilium virorum decernimus et mandamus (We the oft mentioned princes Ramón and Adalmodis, with the advice and aid of our good men, decree and order. . . .).

[76] Ballesteros, II, p. 633.

[77] Item statuerint principes ut exorquiae nobilium videlicet et magnatum tam militum quam burgensium omni tempore in principum potestatem deveniant, videlicet omnia eorum alodia qua quod principi placuit legis habet vigorem. De nobilibus vero illorum faciant ipsi exorqui quecumque voluerint, tam parentibus quam ecclesiis sive pro animabus illorum ea tribuant (Likewise the princes decree that the property of the nobles dying without direct heirs, as well as that of the magnates, soldiers and burgesses should come into the possession of the princes, as should all their allodial property, according to the

the Justinian principle with the old tradition due to influences which shall be explained later in this essay.

---

principle that what pleases the prince has the force of law. Concerning the nobles also let them (lacking direct heirs) make their heirs whomsoever they wish, their parents or the Church for the repose of their souls).

SPANISH MEDIEVAL SIEGE

Chapter IV

Las Siete Partidas and the Influence of the Roman Justinian Law

THE Forum Iudiciorum satisfied the needs of the Spanish people until the days of Don Ferdinand III. During the troubled days of the Reconquest it was not to be expected that new codes could be drawn up. Not that the people felt the lack of these as modern peoples might, for codes of law to them, it should never be forgotten, were primarily codes of principles of justice, and these being deemed eternally true were always apt and sufficient for the various relations that tied together the medieval society of that time. As the Spanish power recovered in its struggle against the Moorish invasions, towns became populated, new towns were formed and country districts were settled. With the conquered Moors and the conquering Spaniards taking up peaceful relations, trade and agriculture flourished.

To arrange all the new relations created by these conditions, the principles of the Forum Iudiciorum and old customs were taken as guides, sometimes the Iberian,[1] sometimes the Roman, sometimes the Visigothic.[2] *Fueros* were granted, not as would be the arbitrary creations customary with modern legislatures, but as spontaneous developments out of the necessities of the times with a view to regulate

---

[1] Hinojosa, E. de, *Estudios sobre la Historia del Derecho español*, Madrid, 1903.
[2] Idem, *El Elemento Germánico en el Derecho español*, Madrid, 1915, pp. 10-15. The sources of customary Germanic law may be studied in the *fueros* of the tenth century and in the territorial law.

the various political, social, economic relations of the people that arose as the societies grew.[3] The Jewish, Moorish or Mudejar populations were ruled by personal law.[4] The norms of the *fueros* derived from the existing practices of the times, the Forum Iudiciorum and the usus terrae. Geographical and political conditions determined the transfer of one *fuero* from one people to another, sometimes changing only the name of the town and ignoring the original conditions under which it was drawn up in the first instance.[5] Gradually thus many *fueros* crystallized into codes, on the model of that of Cuenca. This contains, including the explanations, some nine hundred articles. In studying the *fueros* of the eleventh and twelfth centuries it can be noted that the nucleus was ordinarily the original *fuero* stated briefly as a rule, then the various confirmations and additions, never however voiding the original grant. The lengthy wording was sometimes due to the necessity of arranging compromises between the contending parties.[6]

An interesting treatment of the origin of the *fueros* and the derivations of the word may be found in *Las Siete Partidas, Primera Partida, título* II, which deals with use, custom and *Fuero*. According to the prologue these three are considered the sanctions behind the laws and are derived one from the other, embodying the natural law. Thus use comes from time, custom from use, and *fuero* from custom; that is, use is the practice of actions, custom is the unwritten right (*derecho*), born from practice, and *fuero* is the custom reduced to writing. The gloss of López, following Albericus, says that use differs from custom in that use signifies an act that has been done, and custom the ius (lex 1). But use

[3] Hinojosa, E. de, *Estudios sobre la Historia del Derecho español*, pp. 36-7.
[4] Fernandez y Gonzales, *Estado social y político de los Mudejares en Castilla*, Madrid, 1867.
[5] Hinojosa, Ibid., pp. 31-2.
[6] Ibid., p. 35.

should be introduced without any harm, for the common good, and should not be secret and hidden, but public, so that all men may know it and assent to it (lex 2). The *fuero* is called ius from use (usus), whence *fuero* is derived from forum because it is public and manifest (lex 8). The gloss of López says that forus itself is a general term, and in those things which concern the decision of lawsuits, as is clear from the forum of laws. Improperly then is the municipal forus called a *fuero*, as the *fuero* of Sepúlveda. Another explanation has it that the *fuero* should be open and public, from which it has the name forus. The ancients use the term forum, a place for buying and selling, open to all, whence the name, and since in Spain, business is done publicly, so should the *fuero* be open and public.

Though it was the economic interest that most frequently brought forth the *fuero*, political and administrative institutions were being gradually formed. All the *fueros* recognized that the king was the supreme head of the land, but as the relations regulated by the *fueros* became more complicated, discords and conflicts arose, and the difficulties of administration increased. Hence Don Ferdinand III, who had united Castile and León, wished to have a unified code. During the last years of his reign he initiated the *Fuero Real de España.*[7] The prologue repeats the traditional Spanish conception of the duty of the king,—to end discords, to establish his people in justice, peace and right so that the people may know how to live.[8] It was carried to completion under Don Alfonso X (1254-5), and is more a work of reduction and compilation than a work of science, comprising the most important laws of the *fueros, municipios,* the Forum

[7] Ballesteros, III, p. 432.

[8] For a discussion of the texts and manuscripts, see *Los Códigos Españoles,* I, pp. 429-40.

Iudiciorum and the customs of Castile, and reflecting the influence of the Roman law then so much studied.

Don Alfonso X also had the *Espéculo* or *Espejo de todos los derechos* drawn up, which for many is the precursor of the *Las Siete Partidas.*[9] This task was undertaken by the archbishops, bishops and persons most learned in the law of the times, and illustrates Roman law tendencies. Many of the Spanish jurists had studied at Bologna and at Paris, and had become enamored of the ordered simplicity and comprehensive scope of the Justinian code. Bringing back to Spain their enthusiasm, they gradually gave shape to the idea that a Spanish code should be drawn up on this model. Salamanca in the thirteenth century established a chair of Roman law, and three for the Decretals. At the beginning of the fourteenth century these chairs were increased to four for the Roman law and six for the Decretals. There was only one chair for the teaching of the national law and jurisprudence.[10] All during the thirteenth century, attention was centered upon the Roman law. An inventory of books made in 1273 for Don Gonzalo Palomeque, canon of Toledo [11] lists the Decretals with commentary of Bernardus, the Summa of Gaufridus, the Summa of Azo, the Institutes (with and without commentaries), the Digest, the Code of Justinian, the Commentaries of Innocent on the new Decretals, an Avicenna, Aristotle's De Natura, which gives an idea of the sources consulted at this time. And it is worthy of note that in the glosses made by Gregorio López for *Las Siete Partidas,* these authorities, especially Azo and Innocent, are frequently quoted.

---

[9] Ballesteros, III, p. 432. Menéndez y Pelayo, following Martínez Marina, considers this a falsification of the *Partidas* in order to favor the partisans of Don Sancho IV. For text, consult *Los Códigos Españoles,* VI.

[10] *Los Códigos Españoles,* II, p. xvii.

[11] Martínez-Marina, F., *Ensayo histórico crítico sobre la antiqua legislación. . . . las Siete Partidas,* Madrid, 1808, p. 7, n. 3. Also *Partida* I, *Tít.* I, *leyes* 2, 6.

Don Alfonso himself, however, was not anxious for the ideas current in Bologna and Paris. He wished a full and complete code to be drawn up, which would resolve all the contradictions in the existing codes, but be based upon the good *fueros* and customs of Castile and León, that law which is most common and advantageous throughout the whole world, the holy fathers, decretals and famous jurists.[12] His compilers trained in the new fashions in legal studies, forgot this advice, and produced a code, in the words of Martínez-Marina,[13] "as if they were foreigners in their attitude towards the national jurisprudence, ignorant of the law of their fatherland and of the excellent municipal laws, the good *fueros* and beautiful and praiseworthy customs of Castile and León, and forgetful of and ignoring the wishes of the sovereign who always desired to conserve in the new code, the ancient usages and laws in so far as they were compatible with the principles of justice and public felicity. Not knowing any other source, nor any treasures of erudition and civil and ecclesiastical doctrine than the Decretals, Digest and Code, together with the opinions of the glossators, they introduced into the *Partidas* the Roman legislation and the opinions of its interpreters, altering and amending all our constitution, civil and ecclesiastical, in the most essential points with notable injury to society and the rights and regalia of our sovereign."

It is true that with this code we find introduced new interpretations and new views which as they filtered into the national mind, evolved a new interpretation of the national tradition and ended by swinging Spain away from her proper line of development.

Don Ferdinand III had intended to call his new code by

---

[12] Ibid., p. 7.
[13] Ibid., p. 273.

the title *Setenario,* because he wished to form a harmony and the number seven was considered by the ancients to have mystical significance in this respect. But it would seem that the code as finally compiled between 1256-65 under Don Alfonso X, was originally known as the *Libro de las Leyes,* or *Fuero de las Leyes.*[14] The editors were Jácome or Jacobo Ruiz de las Leyes, chief editor, who was responsible for the third *Partida* and who was a judge, enjoying the confidence of the king and carrying out many delicate missions for him; Fernando Martínez, canon and archdeacon of the Church of Zamora, chaplain and notary of the king in Castile; and Roldán, who had a great reputation for his knowledge of the law.[15] The code was divided into seven books or parts, and hence jurists of the fourteenth century began to call it *Las Siete Partidas* or *Leyes de Partidas.* Oldrado, the famous jurist who lived at the beginning of the reign of Don Alfonso XI, was the first to make this division. Sotelo, in his *Historia del derecho real de España,* holds that the original title was *Libro de las Postruras,*[16] and Espinosa, with others, considers it more likely that it was called the *Septenario.*[17] However this may be, it is now commonly known as *Las Siete Partidas.*

It was not popularly received, owing to the Roman innovations, and Don Alfonso never had the resolution to promulgate it solemnly. It had tremendous influence on the jurists and magistrates who studied it and absorbed its principles. Don Alfonso XI gave it official approval in the *Cortes* of Alcalá in 1348. From then on its principles made great headway. The Roman influence received further im-

---

[14] Ibid., p. 256, n. 1.
[15] Ibid., pp. 263-7. Ballesteros, III, p. 433, adds also Gonzalvo, Archdeacon of Toledo, Juan Alfonso, Archdeacon of Santiago and notary for the king in León, and various lawyers of the University of Salamanca.
[16] Martínez-Marina, p. 257, n. 1.
[17] Ibid., p. 259.

petus from the will of Cardinal Albornoz who died in 1367, leaving funds to establish the college of San Clemente for Spanish students at the University of Bologna.[18]

During the reigns of Don Juan II and of Don Enrique IV, many complaints about the confusion and delays introduced into the laws by the study of the Roman law are on record. The Roman code, digests and decretals became the chief books, and the favorite authorities were Azo, Acusio, Enrique Ostiense, Especulador, Juan Andrés, Bartolus, Baldo, Abad. These oracles are frequently quoted by Gregorio López in his edition of *Las Siete Partidas.*[19] The following verses from Fernán Martínez de Burgos in his *Crónica de Don Alonso VIII,*[20] are typical of the public opinion:

Alcaldes, notarios, é aun oidores
Segund bien creo, pasan de setenta,
Que estan en trono de emperadores
A quien el rey paga infinita renta;
De alios doctores hay ciento y noventa
Que traen el regno entero burlado
E en quarenta anos non es acabado
Un solo pleito mirad si es tormento.

Viene el pleyto a disputacion,
Alte es Bartolo e Chino Digesto
Juan Andres e Baldo, Enrique; de son
Mas opiniones que ubas en cesto;

---

18 For a bibliography of editors and commentators on the *Partidas*, see Ballesteros, III, p. 432, 467.

19 Martínez-Martina, p. 385-7. Consult also the Law of Don Juan II in the Cortes of Toro, 1427, and Law xxvi in the *Cortes* of Briviesca, 1387, relying on Justinian.

20 Quoted by Martínez-Marina, pp. 388-9. Somewhat freely translated, these run as follows: There are alcaldes, notaries and even *oidores* (judges), as I well believe, to the number of more than seventy, around the throne of the emperors, to whom the king pays infinite tribute; of other doctors there are one hundred and ninety, who drag the kingdom into complete ridicule. In forty years not a single lawsuit has been finished; look! if it is not a torment indeed. Should the lawsuit come to court, high is the authority of Bartolus, and the Digest of Chino, Juan Andrés, Baldo and Enrique. There are more opinions than grapes in a basket. And neither lawyer is in any great hurry. As soon as it is seen that the lawsuit is hotly disputed, it fails on a technicality.

E cada abozado es ni mucho presto
E desque bien visto bien disputado
Faltan el pleyto en un punto errado
E torman de cabo a question por esto.

Las Siete Partidas is considered by many as the first true Spanish code, but this is not correct, taking code in its modern sense. It is not only a series of laws, but also a statement of principles,[21] centering around and aiming to extend in the magnificent Roman style, the two great Spanish ideas: Justice is the end and aim of civil society; the king is the mouthpiece of this justice, the gubernator or pilot of his people, responsible to them and to God. It preserves the splendid sweep of the Augustinian theory, that the people are bound together in a union of hearts, interests and wills, into a pactum societatis which creates reciprocal engagements, recognized rights and accepted duties,[22] and analyzed the resulting obligations and sacrifices as they must work out in relation to God, "Who is the beginning, middle and end of all things and without Him nothing can be; through His power are things made, through His wisdom governed, through His goodness maintained,"[23] and also in relation to the sovereign.

At the same time there is the tendency to tie down the interpretation to the strict Graeco-Roman ideal, to each one his due. The glow from the City of God begins to fade, and as time passes Spanish thought and Spanish procedure harden into the formalism which strikes foreign observers as cold and rigid. It is furthermore an indication that Spanish ideas are congealing in a formula at the time when Spain was confronted with the practical application of the Roman

[21] Ballesteros, III, pp. 433-4.
[22] Combès, *La Doctrine Politique de St. Augustin,* Paris, 1927, p. 78.
[23] Opening of the Prologue.

law theories (by peoples who were not Romans), in the midst of economic conditions created by the discoveries of the New World and its civilization.

The reason for this is obvious, once the point is grasped on which turned the conflict between the tradition of the Roman law and that of the Spanish. Justice defined in the sense of "to each one his due," did not satisfy the Roman lawyers. It must be brought out of the realm of individual claims into that of public power. But having the due or right, the possession was absolute and the source of his rights then was within the individual. If this due should be denied him, he could reclaim it by exerting his will. Observing a similarity in the laws of the peoples conquered by Rome, the lawyers assumed a similarity of principle and thus arrived at a notion of a general law prevailing among mankind. All human acts were to be interpreted in terms of will, and justice in the abstract becomes nothing but will. Stoic thought, however, tried to transcend this and evolve a philosophy of justice which would not so obviously need the support of force. The explanation of this general accord lay in universal nature. As Cicero observed, real justice has no existence except by nature. There is but one essential right which binds society together, which one law establishes. This law is right reason and Divine reason must necessarily be possessed of a power to determine what is virtuous and what is vicious. The source then becomes higher than mere gratuitous human force. But the Stoic philosopher in analyzing his concept of reason, traveled around in a circle. Reason is that force which accounts for the order of things, and is at bottom considered but a function of the will.[24]

---

[24] Origin of Sound Democratic Principles in Catholic Tradition, Rev. Moorhouse I. X. Millar, S.J., in "Thought," March, 1928.

With Augustine, the source of justice is God, and the legislator can only hope to write justice into his decisions in proportion as he attains through wisdom to a knowledge of God's will.[25] In other words, the motive force of society will be the individual, as with the Stoics, but an individual maintaining clearly his relations to God and in the light of these conceiving his relations to his neighbors. That this view was deeply impressed upon the Spanish mind is very evident in the Code of the Indies, and certainly not absent from *Las Siete Partidas*, in spite of all the glosses from the Romans. But the seeds introduced here, as we shall show, bore fruit for Spain in the eighteenth and nineteenth centuries and partly contributed to the loss of her colonies. Her phraseology was that of Augustine, but her interpretation was Stoic. She felt the pull of her old tradition, she tried to think the thought of her new interpretation. In the face of her enemies who had long since forgotten the old Augustinian tradition which they once had shared in common with Spain but had failed to develop, and who were therefore freer to pursue their ill-regulated ends and ambitions with an undivided mind, Spain was helpless. Her revenge, in the grand style so dear to the hearts of her courteous people, may lie in the preservation of her great codes in the study of which her enemies may be led to regain the light to save them from the fate which is overtaking them.

Certainly all who ponder over *Las Siete Partidas*, whether jurists, philosophers, or *littérateurs*, find it a work of exquisite and laborious erudition,[26] and are enchanted by its eloquent, majestic style, its admirable order and wisdom, its harmonious disposal of the complicated relationships of life

[25] Combès, Ibid., pp. 138-9.
[26] Martínez-Marina, op. cit., p. 271.

and its clear statement of principles,[27] though the *Cortes* of 1447 found some of the laws obscure and doubtful. Of the twenty printed editions up to 1847, only three are important,[28] and the best of these is that edited by Gregory López of the Council of the Indies, in the sixteenth century. So many demands were made for an accurate and authoritative edition, that Lorenzo Galindez de Cárbajal and Gregorio López began its revision. The *Cortes* of Madrid, 1552, requested a new edition also. Cárbajal's edition was not printed, but López' first edition appeared at Salamanca in 1555. It was submitted to the *Consejo real* by order of the king, before being printed. A *cédula* of Doña Juana, dated September 7, 1555, declared this edition authentic and ordered a copy to be placed in the archives of Simancas, and also requested that if any one should have any doubt of the text, or any part of the text, he deposit his version, printed, in the said archives.[29] The Salamanca edition was the first to receive official approval and is famous for the correctness of the text and the glosses of López, which reflect the views current in the sixteenth century and are of great interest as showing the progress in the acceptance of the Roman interpretations since 1265. López does not give the manuscripts from which he made his corrections, probably thinking that since his work was to have official sanction, it was not necessary. Twelve editions have been based upon his, those of 1565, 1576, 1587, 1765, 1843 including his glosses.[30] López was considered to have written

[27] For an account of the various editions, see the Introduction, written by Gómez de la Serna, Vol. II, pp. xxxvi-xlvi, of *Los Códigos Españoles*.

[28] The first edition was brought out in 1491 by Alonzo Diaz de Montalvo, the distinguished jurist of the fifteenth century, who published at the order of the Catholic Kings, the *Fuero real,* and compiled the *Ordenanzas reales de Castilla.* He was advanced in years and almost blind, hence his edition is full of errors, mutilated clauses and printer's mistakes, possibly due to the newness of the art of printing and to the importation of foreign printers. It remained the text for six further editions.

[29] *Los Códigos Españoles,* II, p. xxxvi, for text of the *cédula.*

[30] The edition quoted in this essay is in *Los Códigos Españoles,* vols. II, III, IV. It follows the Salamanca edition of 1555 with the typographical errors corrected according

a golden book and he is held up as an oracle, but it is to be remembered that in general he explains the Spanish law in terms of Roman and canon law, not dwelling on those that did not specially fall in with the views of his age. He was not, however, ignorant of the long Spanish tradition going back to the days of Isidore, and all his comments are worthy of careful study. It should also be borne in mind that since the days of St. Isidore, Spain had turned out a long list of scholars, the like of which few nations in Europe can match for the same period of time. The sixteenth century, López' century, produced a galaxy of theologians and jurists whose learning was of such comprehensive and cosmopolitan character, that it is very difficult for students to pick out from the mass of their writings their own particular views, seeing that they surveyed their subject with such complete detachment and from so many and such varied angles.[31]

In the prologue to *Las Siete Partidas*, we find the first hint of the influence of the Roman law. In stating his aims Don Alfonso outlined the traditional view of the kingship. Since justice is the king's concern, he is mindful of the judgments to be passed on his actions, not only by God, from Whose judgment no one in any manner whatsoever may hide or be excused if he doeth ill, but also by the people who more often judge things by will than by right. Hence this book was to show forth the right way of living, to separate right from wrong and to distinguish the lie from the truth, so that all may know the way and that justice may

---

to the edition of Berní y Catalá in Valencia, 1759 and reprinted at Madrid, 1789. Vol. V contains an index, and index of glosses.

It is also to be noted that the edition of the Spanish Academy of History, 1818, to which Martínez-Marina wrote the introduction, later printed separately as the *Ensayo crítico histórico* etc. is full of errors, contains many heretical statements, especially *Partida Primera, título* IV, and is in every way inferior to the edition of López. The king declared this edition to be official. Those who were in charge of the government at this time had little interest in publishing anything that ran contrary to their notions on what was Spanish tradition.

[31] Hinojosa, E. de, *Influencia que tuvieron en el derecho . . . los filósofos y teólogos*, p. 91.

be done, which is none other than the giving to each one what belongs to him, according to what he deserves.[32]

López' gloss on the phrase "the people more often judge things by will than by right", is of interest as showing the views current on the check the people had on the king. He calls attention to the point that the voice of the people is a divine voice, but the voice of the people, especially if aroused and excited, does not make an act just, that is, the justice of an act was something intrinsic and beyond the opinion of anyone. However, he goes on to say, if the people follow something already openly established, they may not be restrained from so doing, and the one who is in the position of the superior ought to yield that the people may rest in peace and the Church be undisturbed; further the superior may change what is established at his discretion, by substituting something equally good or better, but he is not obliged to hold to what is promised because of an outcry of the people, though he is bound to that agreed to in a compact made at the supplication of the people.[33]

A further gloss on the word "right" reminds the reader that the people are not necessarily of sound mind.[34] Hence the responsibility of deciding as to justice lies with the ruler. This reflects the principle of the Forum Iudiciorum, though in this code, this responsibility derives directly from the fact that the king on assuming the kingship automatically re-

---

[32] Cf. Prologue, *Los Códigos Españoles,* II.

[33] The gloss of López reads: vox populi, vox divina. Tumultuosae voces populi si rationi consonant et naturale motivo irritos non faciunt actus iustos. Bald. in rubric. C. si quis aliquem testari prohibit, vel cogerit, col. 10. Quid autem si populus non vult consentire electo per collegium, an irritibatur electio? Gloss. in cap. 1, 62, dist. dicit quod non, ex quo non habet causam rationabilem contradicendi, nisi scandalum generetur. Quod ultimum multum notat Abb. in cap. 1, col. 2 ad fin. De elect. Adduceris etiam notabile dictum Innoc. in cap. nisi cum pridem de renunt. quod si populus persequitur pallatum iam institutum, nec potest compesci a tali persecutione debet praelatus cedere ut populus quiescat, et ecclesia stet in quiete; vel poterit removeri per superiorem assignato sibi alibi bono cambio, quod dicit signanter notandum. Et dixit gloss in cap. unusquisque in parte saltantium 22 quaes. 4 quod promissum ad clamorem populi non tenet; tenebit tamen contractus factus ad preces populi, ut notat gloss in cap. postquam 13, quaest. 2.

[34] Dicit Bald. in 1. Omnes populi, col. 2 ff. de just. et iur. Quod nullus populus est sani capitis et ubi major numerus ibi minus intellectus.

ceives the authority that goes with it. This authority, because it is a participation in the Divine authority, carries with it also a participation of the Divine justice. The principle of the king's justice is thus placed on a higher plane.

A new point of view is also introduced in the gloss on the phrase to show forth to the people the right way of living. López describes jurisprudence as the explanation of things divine and human, the knowledge of that which is just and unjust.[35] But however López and the jurists of his time interpret the divinarum atque humanarum rerum notitia, the Roman lawyers, Caius and Ulpian, did not have the same view, and the wedge here introduced gradually diverted the Spanish interpretations from the traditional connotations of the words.

The contradictions between the two theories come out more clearly in Title I of the first *Partida*, which deals with the subject matter of the laws. In the prologue to this title it is laid down that laws are established that men may know how to live fittingly [36] and to please God and to live in right and in justice with each other. The gloss here interprets the "living well" in the Aristotelian sense and not in the Augustinian, which, supplemented by St. Thomas, included this but goes on further to take in the Christian view of man's final destiny. Thus the way is being paved for a shift in the point from which life is to be viewed.

A further gloss states that this does not lay down a definition of law, but gives the causes.[37] But this is a definition of

[35] Iurisprudentia est divinarum atque humanarum rerum notitia, justi atque injusti scientia, Insti. de just. et iur. in princip.

[36] Quod legalia justa dicimus factiva et conservativa felicitatis et particularium ipsius politica communicatione (Just legislation is framed with a view to establishing and preserving the happiness of the individuals in political communication).

[37] Non ponitur hic legis definitio sed ponuntur causae quae conduntur leges. Est enim lex omnium divinarum atque humanarum rerum notitia, regula iustorum et iniustorum praeceptrix faciendorum, prohibitrix non faciendorum (This does not lay down a definition of law, but sets forth the principles on which laws are founded. For law is the knowledge of things, divine and human, the measure of the just and the unjust, instructing that which is to be done and forbidding that which is not to be done). López wishes his gloss here to be read with the glosses on Laws II and IV.

law as the term had been used in Spanish juridic history. The text of law 1, shows this: Statutae sunt leges iustae, ut inter homines ius et iustitia servetur (Just laws are instituted in order that among men right and justice may be preserved). From the comment at the beginning of this title, it may be inferred that the discussion was going on among the jurists as to what was law. Was law a rule or a form of procedure, laid down by the proper authority, or was it a philosophical statement of principles to be used as a guide for conduct? To follow justice here on earth so as to meet the demands of divine justice hereafter? If so, law should follow the prescriptions of justice and show the way by principles rather than by rules. This was the traditional Spanish view influenced by Augustinian-Platonic conceptions.[38]

In this comment at the head of Title I, it is stated that each title is to contain the explanations of that which is set forth in it and these and such interpretations are called laws. But because the Latin peoples (the Title goes on to say), call laws the beliefs which men have, some would have it that those (explanations) should not speak of anything but these (beliefs) only. But we (that is, the king) in order to draw them out of this doubt, wish to make them understand what laws are, and in what manner they may be distinguished and why they have this name, and what are their virtue, force and source.

Here is seen the attempt made by the Roman trained jurists to reconcile Spanish and Roman theory. There is a philosophy behind each view, but it is not the same philosophy. Gómez de la Serna, commenting on the matter in the preceding paragraph, says that law here is equivalent to right or jurisprudence, the principle of the definition being

[38] In so far as law is the rule of action, made by the proper authority, it was the expression of custom. See Forum Iudiciorum, and Title II of *Partida primera.*

to call that science law which is the knowledge of all things, human and divine. This he considers inexact, and thinks it has its origin in the rivalry between the Stoic philosophers and the Roman jurists, each one attributing to the science which he professed, the power of doing good to man, and for this reason Ulpian defined the science of law in the same terms as the ancient philosophers defined philosophy.[39]

This is not quite correct. It is not to be explained in terms of rivalry. What appealed to the Roman mind was the order implied in and determined by justice. To get a philosophical explanation of this they drew upon the Stoic philosophers, whose chief concern was the naturalis ratio, the objective and external order of nature. Law had to be explained in terms that would go behind the mere laying down and carrying out of a rule of action, necessary as this last might be recognized to be for the organization and prosperity of society. The Stoic supplied this rationalistic explanation in the doctrine of the ius naturalis, that is the justice and reason which had their source in the naturalis ratio. As to the source of this ratio, the Stoic philosophers were not clear (though the Stoic lawyers were forced to a much more definite statement in their doctrine on the law and the function of will in the law); it was sufficient for them (the philosophers), that law, being part of nature and inseparable from reason, was the common patrimony of all humanity.[40]

But Spanish legal thought as has been shown above originated in the doctrines of St. Augustine. He, too, was impressed with the order involved in justice. In fact to him order might be called the first concern of justice. But that order was not merely a distinction between just and unjust, modeled on the "nature" of the Stoic, but that tranquillity

---

[39] See note of de la Serna, *Partida Primera, Título* I, *1.* 1 in *Los Códigos Españoles,* II.
[40] Combès, op, cit., p. 123.

and harmonious accord of souls, which he termed peace (pax). To the Stoic order was impersonal, abstract, immutable; to Augustine it was the equilibrium, harmony, security which comes to the soul when Christ reigns within it. Augustine has thus changed the orientation of justice. It flows from the knowledge of God. This tranquillity which results from the soul being at one with its end, implies conformity with order, consequently justice. From which it follows that the aim of civil society will be to foster the conditions under which it may be attained and the object of laws will be to lay down the principles which may guide to this end.

But to the Stoic law is the force of reason, that right reason given by nature, as stated by Cicero, the most eloquent exponent of the Stoic philosophy,[41] and there is only one rule with which to distinguish a good law from a bad—nature.[42] On the contrary, says St. Augustine, law is reason written naturally in the heart of man [43] and there is no right where there is no justice.[44] Nor can there be justice or legitimacy in the temporal law, which is not derived from the eternal law.[45]

In the second law under this title, the confusion of the two lines of thought is even more clearly visible. The natural law is that common to all living things; the law of nations that which is common to men.[46] This departs from the definition given by St. Isidore, which said: Ius is either natural or civil or universal (ius gentium). Ius naturale is what is common to peoples and what is observed everywhere by

[41] Lex est naturalis vis. De leg., I, 6. Lex est recta ratio a natura data. De. Leg. I, 12, quoted by Combès, p. 131.

[42] Cicero, De Leg., II, 2, quoted ibid., p. 137.

[43] Lex est ratio hominis naturaliter in corde conscripta. Epistola, 157, 15, in P.L., xxxiii, quoted ibid., p. 13.

[44] Ibid., p. 137. De Civ. Dei, xxix, 21.

[45] De Libero arbitrio, I, VI, 15 in P.L., xxxii, 1230.

[46] Est ius naturalis, quod est commune omnibus animantibus, est ius gentium, quod est communis hominibus.

the instinct of nature, rather than by any convention (non constitutione aliqua), as the marriage of man and woman, the begetting of children, the common possessions of all, the one freedom for all, the acquisition of those things that are taken in the air or in the sea or on the land.[47]

The comment of López attempts to make the meaning of this law clear and gives various interpretations of it. He says that therein is described or defined the ius naturalis, as that which is common to men and brutes, which nature teaches all animals [48] (which is the Stoic view). According to this the ius naturalis is instilled into animals by nature, that is by divine disposition, as declares Albericus, but according to the nature which man has in common with the angels (rational), the natural law is defined as a certain reason (ratio) of nature instilled into human beings for the doing of good and the avoiding of evil, from which the first principle of the natural law may be deduced, to do good and avoid evil (quoting St. Thomas).[49] But these interpretations do not all agree. St. Thomas was careful to explain on this same question, the phrase of the Roman lawyers—which nature teaches all animals—bringing out the point that according to nature there are three things to be considered in man. All those things to which man has a natural inclination are naturally apprehended by reason as good, and he therefore seeks good, first as all things in nature must seek that which is necessary for their final end; secondly according to what his own nature possesses in common with other animals, "and in virtue of this inclination those things are said to belong to the natural law, which nature has taught to all animals"; and thirdly in accordance with his reason since rational nature is special

[47] Etymol., Bk. V, cap. 4, 1.
[48] Lex 1, ius naturale ff. de just. et iur. et instit. de iure natur. gent. et civ. in princip.
[49] St. Thomas, I, II, quaest. 94, art. 2, 4, 5.

to him.[50] In other words, behind St. Thomas' explanation is the thought of Aristotle's distinction between that which is natural in the sense of that which is derived from nature and that which is natural in the sense of that which is demanded by nature in view of the final end. The thought of the Stoic philosophers did not go beyond the objective and external order observed in nature which to them was a manifestation of the naturalis ratio, whereas St. Thomas brings out the distinction between laws of nature and natural law.[51] If López grasped St. Thomas' idea he did not follow it up in his gloss, and as time passed, more attention was paid to the Roman philosophy than to the point introduced by the Scholastic interpretation. This diversion of thought from the main issue weakened in the minds of the Spanish jurists the significance of their earlier tradition, to which St. Thomas offered supplementary justification.

Leaving the field of principles, Laws III, IV, V, VI, VII, VIII and X are attempts to develop the definition in what might be called a legal sense as distinct from a philosophical principle, and this introduces another wedge into the Spanish tradition. Laws were principles *of* conduct, not rules *for* conduct. Henceforth they were to be made rules for conduct. This is especially noticeable if one compares the Code of the Indies with that of *Las Siete Partidas.* The Code of the Indies is very much a code of rules and regulations laid down by the king.

Isidore of Seville had distinguished between lex and mos. Lex was the written ordinance, mos, custom approved by antiquity, but unwritten. Lex, derived from legere, to read, is the term used for that which is written.[52] And again lex is the

[50] Summa, I, II, quaest. 94, art. 2.
[51] Zybura, Present Day Thinkers and the New Scholasticism, St. Louis, 1926, pp. 311-20, art. by Rev. Moorhouse I. X. Millar, S.J.
[52] Etymol., Bk. V, cap. 3, 2.

enactment of the people, by which the elders with the people sanction some law.[53] Law permits, forbids or punishes something,[54] but is always an outgrowth of custom. This theory is still the background of the *Partidas,* but interest has shifted to the binding force and to the question of who may make the laws.

In the comment on Law IV,[55] the question is raised as to whether the essence of law is that it should be written. Albericus held that law should be written, but the common opinion is that the character of its being written is accidental, (that is to induce an obligation from the law), since before it was written the law did not bind, and thus rights were not harmonized.

Laws IX, XI and XII (*Primera Partida, Título* I) explain how laws should be made. According to the first two, laws should be carefully thought out, to be certain that justice is contained in them, and to the end that they will serve God, the temporal lords and the common good of all. For this the counsel of learned and just men, having no desire to dominate, is necessary. And the maker of the laws should love God and His justice, and desire the common good. For this he will need training and education, the gloss of López notes.

Law XII reads as follows: The emperor or king in his dominion, or some other by his mandate, may make laws on temporalities.[56] At first glance this would seem to allow much latitude to the king, but the comment brings out the force of the old Spanish traditions. It would appear, says

---

[53] Etymol., Bk. V, 19, 1.

[54] Etymol., Bk. V, 19.

[55] Lex est castigatio seu doctrina scripta reprimens vitam hominis, ne malam faciat et docens quae sunt facienda et dicitur, lex, quia eius praecepta debent esse legalia et Iusta. *Partida primera, Tít.* I, *ley* 4. (Law is the sanction or written instruction restraining the life of man, lest he do evil, and teaching those things which are to be done, and it is called law because its precepts should be legitimate and just.)

[56] Imperator aut rex in dominio suo, vel alius eius mandato potest legam condere super temporalibus.

López, that this law would cover the whole kingdom, since to no other but the king is given the power of making laws. Nevertheless if there be particular statutes applying to places, towns or entities of the kingdom, this law has no bearing on them. They will remain therefore in the disposition of the common right, according to which, by many laws, it is permitted to the people to establish statutes, whence it follows that dukes, counts, marquises, or any other of the lords, may not in their lands enact laws without the consent of the people. On the contrary, that law establishes what they (the lords) may do in accordance with the consent of the people, and as has been said above, validates the statute made by the people, not by the duke or count, and the lord may intervene only in so far as his magisterial authority extends. This is the interpretation to be put upon the statement of those who say that in the enactments of the statutes of the people, a higher authority is necessary.[57] That the people may make statutes, even lacking jurisdiction, is the more common view of the legists and canonists, such as Albericus, Alexander, and Balduinus. The last mentioned holds that in a statute or ordinance of the people, the consent of the prince is not required, but the authority of their own magistrate and the general freedom which all the people have suffice. There may be limitations upon this power in regard to penal laws (unless held by custom through a special privilege), or in the decision of cases (reserved to Bishops), or on questions of administration of public affairs, proposed laws or amendments on these being reserved for consultation with the prince, according to the royal *Ordenamiento*.[58]

---

[57] Albericus, L, Omnes populi, col 9 in princip.

[58] E si vieren que algunas ordenanzas se deben desfacer, o emendar, las farán de nuevo, con acuerdo del regimiento mirando mucho á las que tocaren a le eleccion de los oficios para que se eligan justamente sin parcialidad asimismo las que conciernen al bien común, así en que los menestrales, é otros oficiales usen de sus oficios bien, é fielmente sin fraude alguno, como en que la tierra sea bien bastecida, de carnes, e

Moreover if the prince should be within the city, his authority is required.[59] Also the people may not enact statutes against the common right of the kingdom, for over such they have no power, according to Jacob de Are, on the ground that if an equal among equals may not make laws, how much less may the inferior make a law against that of the superior, (though Albericus does not agree with him).

López, however, rejects the view of Albericus, since this is to weaken the power of the kingdom and obedience to the laws. Nor is it likely that the emperor would give to all the people such power as would bring into contempt his own laws. Even Albericus could not deny this, since he holds that the emperor has the check in his hand and may revoke all the statutes of the people. Certainly it is more correct to hold that in general the law is binding upon all the people, that they may not do anything against this law of the emperor, which is not in accordance with the common right. Nor could any prince concede such a power, for Angel in his "Imperium" (col. 2 ff. de iurisdictione omni judic.) holds that the making of laws is an attribute of the supreme power (imperium) which belongs to the prince alone as part of his function (competit). Lucas de Penna (in L. Contra publicam, col. 4, 5, c. de re militari, lib. 12), raises the question whether the people might introduce custom against the law of the prince. López considers a sufficient answer to this may

---

pescados e otros mantenimientos a razonables precios, é que las calles e carreras e carrecerias esten limpias, e que las salidas del lugas esten asi limpias e desocupados: e las ordenanzas que ansi enmendaren o de nuevo hicieren, envien a nos el traslado de ellas para que nos las mandemos veer a proveer sobre ellos (And if they see that some ordinances should be revised or amended, they will make them anew, with the agreement of the government, looking well to those things which touch the election of officials in order that they may be selected justly without partiality, and also to those things which concern the common good; also whether the *menestrales* (certain judges), and other officials, carry out their duties, well and faithfully and without any fraud, whether the land may be stocked with meat and fish and other supplies at reasonable prices, whether the streets, roadways and paths, be clean, whether the outlets of the public places be clean and open. Copies of the ordinances which thus they may amend or initiate, shall be sent to us in order that we may order them to be inspected and approved).

[59] *Cortes* of Valladolid, 1537, pet. 28.

be found in the following law: [60] Inducitur consuetudo ex usu populi per tempus decem et viginti annorum, sciente domino et non contradicente, et si dicto tempore bis fuerit per eum judicatum vel si in judicio contra eam non fuerunt rationes per eam judicatum vel fuit judicatum pro ea. Item non debet irrationabilis, vel contra ius naturale seu bonum commune, nec per errorem debet introduci quia alias esset corruptela et non teneret.[61]

The gloss of López on this brings out the interesting point that in some places, all men, in others the greater part, may induce custom, and in the cities ruled by decurions, the latter as representing the people may do so. Albericus holds that one-fourth of the people is sufficent to induce custom for the civil law, if the custom has been used for from ten to twenty years, for canon law, forty years is necessary; and if it is to prevail against the prince, it must have been in use from time immemorial. Two judgments must be given on it, and López says that in all the manuscripts, and he consulted many, at least thirty judges must advise on it.

Evidently the point at issue in this discussion is the sovereignty of the people versus the sovereignty of the king. In the Roman law, the sovereignty (imperium) was vested in the prince or ruler, and hence what the prince ruled was law since "the people make over to him their whole power and authority." [62] This however removes law making from the field of reason to that of will.

To the Spanish mind sovereignty was authority to rule, but authority informed and checked by the end for which

[60] *Primera Partida, Titulo* II, *ley* 5.

[61] Custom may be induced by the use of the people through a period of thirty years, the lord having knowledge of it and not opposing it, and if during the said period, there will have been two judgments on it, or if in judgments against it the reasons have not been admitted, or if judgments are passed in favor of it. Likewise, it should not be unreasonable, against the natural law or the common good; nor should it be introduced through error since it then would corrupt others and it would not hold.

[62] Origin of Sound Democratic Principles in Catholic tradition, Rev. Moorhouse I. X. Millar, S.J., in "Thought" for March, 1928, p. 600.

it was set up. The early medieval Spanish mind approached the problem through the argument that since to secure justice was the aim of civil society, there must necessarily be some one person who would have the charge and the responsibility of seeing that justice was accomplished. And to this person must be given the power to make the laws necessary to achieve this end. It might be said that justice was the juridic origin of his power, in virtue of the fact that justice is the plan by which God governs His universe. It was fitting that one should have this power, and the favorite analogy here was to compare society to the body,—one principle rules it, the soul commands the body, reason directs the passions.[63] This was the Augustinian view.

St. Augustine as a philosopher and an idealist, poet and mystic, looked upon society as an example of, a mirror of, the Divine Justice and thus placed things on a very high plane. But he was none the less mindful of earthly things. His scheme did not contemplate leaving the king to himself in the interpretation of his duty. And both the Forum Iudiciorum and the *Partidas* stress that the king should never exercise the law-making power without consulting the wise men of his kingdom, nor should he set aside laws or change them without reasonable cause, which was interpreted to mean anything against the common good or justice.[64]

Nor had the king any power to legislate arbitrarily. Use or custom was the source of all law and the king could not do more than see that justice as determined by him was enforced in regard to these.[65] The people themselves might

---

[63] Cf. Contra Julianum, IV, 61 in P.L., xlv, 767-8. Also St. Thomas, De Regimine, Lib. I, c. xii.

[64] *Partida Primera, Tít.* I, *leyes* xvii, xiv and xviii. and glosses on these. Justice, in the medieval sense, was meant, and included anything against the laws of God, against known good, and against the sovereignty of the king. In case of dispute, or a question of two evils, decision was to be made for the thing nearest to good.

[65] Usus in hac materia consuetudinis est id quod oritur ex dictis et factis, quae homines populi dicunt et faciunt, sequuntur continuatim longi temporis spatio, metu vel coactione aliqua non interveniente (The practice in the matter of custom is this, that it arises from

originate custom.[66] The one on whom kingship was conferred was chosen by the people, that is by those whom custom had agreed on as the ones suitable to act for the people, the clergy, the rich men (that is men whose substantial position in the society gave them weight and influence), the great nobles, officials of the court, who by their standing in the state might be expected to give wise counsel and make a good choice.[67] The monarchy had become hereditary before the time of the *Partidas* as a natural development of the times.

Under the Asturian monarchy there did not exist a law of succession to the crown, though it appears that the monarchy was elective, following the Visigothic practice. There was a tendency on the part of some of the kings to suggest their successors, as when Don Alfonso II of Castile had his cousin Don Ramiro recognized, or when Don Ordoño I was associated with his father in the work of government, and when Don Ferdinand I delegated some of the task of government to his three sons. According to Pellicer and Mariana, Don Pelayo, the first king of the Reconquest, regulated the succession in a law or testament, basing this opinion on some manuscripts of the *Crónica* of Lucas de Tuy. The existence

---

deeds and words, the things which people say and do and which endure continuously through a long period of time, with no hindrance either from fear or coaction), *Partida Primera, Tít.* II, *ley* 1.

Ubi lex non disponit admittitur consuetudo et consuetudo est legum interpres, et corregit ius anterius si est generalis si specialis in illo loco dumtaxat ubi servatur si princeps scit, ne contradicat intra 10-20 annos. Item tollitur consuetudo per contrariam consuetudinem posteriorem aut legem (Where the law does not settle the matter, custom is admitted, and custom is the interpreter of the law, and corrects the anterior ius, if it is general; if it is special in that place, then only where it is held will it have this effect if the prince knows it and does not contradict it within ten to twenty years. Likewise, custom is destroyed through a contrary posterior custom or a law), *Partida Primera, Tít.* II, *ley* 6.

[66] Quinque modis introducitur consuetudo. Primus, si fiat de re, ex qua bonum potest sequi. Secundum si fiat publice et cum concilio. Tertius, si fiat cum omnium voluntate majorum et minorum. Quartus, quod non fiat contra iura. Quintus quod fiat mandato vel permisione domini (There are five ways in which custom may be introduced. First, if it be done from a thing from which good may follow. Secondly, if it be done publicly and with advice. Thirdly, if it be done by the will of all, the great and the least. Fourthly, if it be not done against right, and fifthly, it may be done by the command or with the permission of the lord). Ibid., *ley* 6.

[67] Ballesteros, II, pp. 282-4.

of this has been much discussed by historians, and denied by Luis de Molina (De primogeniorum hispanorum origine ac natura) and Ambrosio de Morales (*Crónica de España*). Ureña y Smenjaud [68] publishes the Latin text of what he considers to be this law. He found it inserted in the Titulus Primus De electione principum, cap. IX, on the Codex Matritense 772 and cap. XII on the Codex Matritense 12924 (of the sixteenth century). Whether a true document or a forgery, it does represent the ideas according to which the order of succession was finally settled.

That the hereditary succession did not preclude the idea of choice upon the part of the people, is clear from the coronation ceremonies. Ballesteros [69] describes a ceremonial at the end of the twelfth century. On the day appointed, a Sunday, the clergy and people assembled at the palace of the future king and from there proceeded to the Church. The Archbishop led the procession to the choir, all intoning the Domine salvum fac regem. Here the king laid aside his robe and arms and conducted by two bishops approached the altar. After the singing of the Litany of the Saints, the Archbishop questioned the prince. Do you wish to preserve the Holy Faith the Catholic holy men have delivered to you, and to persevere in just works? I wish it, responded the prince. Do you wish to be the guard and defender of the holy churches and their ministers? I wish it, replied the prince. Do you wish to rule and govern the kingdom, which God has granted to you conformably to the justice of your ancestors? I do wish it, again replied the prince, And in so far as you can, relying on Divine aid and on the aid of all your

[68] Opus cit., Appendix IV, pp. 548-51. See also note 6, page 45 of this essay.

[69] II, p. 488, quoting from Sánchez Albornez, *La Sucesion al trono* in *La Monarquia en Asturias, León y Castilla, durante la Alta media,* a manuscript in the library of the Faculty of *Filosofía y Letras* of the *Universidad Central* of Madrid.

faithful men—do you promise to work faithfully in all things?

Then the prelate, turning towards the people, said, Do you wish to submit yourselves to such a prince and ruler and to confirm his kingdom, to establish it with firm faith, to obey his mandates according to that saying of the Apostle, Each soul is subject to the highest powers and to that of the king as the most excellent? The people and clergy answered, So be it, so be it, amen. Then the Archbishop annointed the king, handing him the scepter of authority and crowning him.

But however chosen, the king was not considered to have his authority from the people. That went with the position. This is the key note of the whole theory of the kingship but it is hardly ever recognized or given its full significance in the development of institutions. As the philosophers were more studied, particularly Aristotle, the Roman lawyers and St. Thomas, especially the De Regimine, new ideas on the share of the people in government, and more definite conception of the forms government might take, were introduced into Spanish thought.

We see the conflict of these ideas reflected in the glosses of López on Law XI. The Roman law had gained the greater weight by his time and thus the Spanish were insensibly turned from the logical development of their own theory to the acceptance of a theory already developed on alien principles and to the attempt to read these into a Christian tradition. The Spaniards had objected strenuously to the new principles when the code was first made public, but as it was read, digested and applied by the lawyers, the principles were adopted despite the people. Nevertheless the study of the glosses of López shows how slow this process was and how the effort was made to reconcile the pagan and the Christian, generally by using the pagan when the vocabulary sounded the same.

This tendency is illustrated in the first law of the first title of the second *Partida,* which treats of the imperial power, royal dignity and power in general. This begins: The dignity of ruling is the greatest and most exalted above other temporal dignities, and the king and the emperor to whom, according to right and the assent of the people belongs the direction of the empire. . . .[70] The gloss says: For the lord to whom God gives such honor is the king and emperor, to him belongs by right the grant which the people made anciently to govern and maintain the empire in justice. López quotes in support of this the Institutes and Cicero, partim ense et partim consensu. Nor was this unjust, for the Romans raised up their imperium by their virtues, and it would seem as if their dominion was approved and legitimate, conferred on them by God[71] as may be seen from the De Civitate Dei of St. Augustine (V) and the De Regimine of St. Thomas (lib. III).

In this section of the De Civitate Dei, St. Augustine was discussing the Romans from a different point of view entirely. He was elaborating his philosophy of history, and treating the Romans and their empire in their setting in the whole scheme of things according to his own conception of the City of God. He was defending himself from the charge of condemning them and trying to establish that they had a place in the Divine plan inasmuch as by their stern and lofty virtues (of which he gives examples from their earlier history), they deserved to rule, and in this sense shared in the great work of showing forth the justice of God. But he was

[70] Imperii dignitas maxima est, et aliis dignitatibus temporalibus excellentior; his Rex est Imperator, cui secundum ius et populi assensum competit imperii gubernatio. . . .

[71] Quod Romani virtutibus promuerunt imperium. et diffinire videtur eorum dominium fuisse legitimum et eis a Deo collatum.

not in this connection concerned with the origin of sovereignty and its implications. As a matter of fact he emphatically condemned the Roman idea of dominion and imperium.

In the third book of the De Regimine,[72] after showing that all dominion is from God, first from the nature of being, from creation and from the final end, the author takes up the case of the Romans. He holds that since all dominion is from God, He inspired the Romans to rule well, which they did, and thus deserved their empire, and he follows practically the same arguments as St. Augustine.[73]

In both cases the thought is the same: all authority is from God, and the rulers share in it, inasmuch as they are the ones to carry out the purposes of God in respect to His justice, though the De Regimine is more deductive in the reasoning. Neither was thinking in terms of the author of the Institutes who explained that the emperor had his power because the people handed it over to him.

The confusion of thought is even greater in the gloss on the following law which takes up the subject of what belongs to the sovereignty of the emperor.[74] The discussion here turns on whether the powers granted to the emperor might be taken away or not and is treated from the point of view of what the Romans did, and it is difficult to decide whether he had in mind the Holy Roman Empire or the ancient empire. As far as the Holy Roman Empire was concerned, López or any other Spaniard, would not hold that Spain was under its jurisdiction in any way whatsoever.[75] As for the ancient Romans, López quotes Bartolus (L. Hostes, col. 1,

[72] This was not written by St. Thomas, but by Ptolomeus of Lucca.

[73] De Regimine, Lib. III, cap. I-VI.

[74] *Partida Segunda, Tit.* I. *ley* 2.

[75] After the Council of Florence in 1065, report was made to Don Ferdinand that Spain was subject to the emperor. He denied this, consulted with his councils and on advice of the Cid, claimed that neither the Emperor, nor anyone else, had jurisdiction over Spain, since none had aided against the Moors. This was sent to the Pope. The Legate and the Ambassadors discussed it at Toulouse, and decision was rendered in favor of Spain. Mariana, *Historia general de España.*

2ff and others [76] to the effect that to him to whom belongs the power to institute belongs also the power to destroy. All things are dissolved in their causes. On this ground the Romans disposed of Tarquin. On the other hand the same Bartolus holds that the transfer of power made by the Roman people to the emperor was in the nature of a reciprocal agreement, "or a certain tacit contract between the people and the emperor, and once taken up by the emperor, it does not seem as if any withdrawal on the part of the people would be admitted." [77] The foregoing view loses sight entirely of the traditional Spanish idea of the monarchy, and introduces the theory of absolutism which later was taken up by the kings and people alike.

Others again (continues the gloss) hold that the empire (imperium) is from the ordinance of the Church, rather than by suffrage of the people, and the Pope alone could depose the emperor for grave reasons.[78] Others again were of the opinion that if the king were a tyrant, he could be set aside by the same multitude which made the pact with him, as St. Thomas holds in the De Regimine.[79] The Spanish tradition on this point will be taken up later. Enough has been said here to show how confusion was being introduced into the Spanish theory of government through the influence of the Roman law principles. The Spanish went on to develop their administrative institutions without realizing the modifications made in their principles, until they found themselves with a set of institutions not to their liking, but they did not then know how to extricate themselves out of their dilemmas.

---

[76] Jacob. Hutii; Erasmus.

[77] Seu quidam contractus innominatus inter populum et imperatorem, et sequuto implemento ex parte imperatoris, non videtur, amittenda poenitentia ex parte populi.

[78] Cap. Venerabilem de elec. cap. ad apostolicae de re judic. lib. 6, Clement Romani Principes de iure, iud. Also Bald. L. fin. c. de legit.

[79] Lib. I, cap. X.

Complaints that the Romanization of *Las Siete Partidas* had brought such a state of confusion by the times of the Catholic Kings, that these commissioned Don Alfonso de Montalvo, a noted jurist, to make a compilation of the most notable laws as early as 1484. This came out as the *Ordenanzas Reales de Castilla,* also called *Ordenamiento de Montalvo,* first printed in Salamanca, 1523, and again in 1779 with the gloss of Diego Perez. It is printed in Volume VI of *Los Códigos Españoles* without the glosses. Doña Isabella requested Montalvo to edit the *Partidas,* which were published at Seville in 1491. Montalvo also glossed the *Fuero Real,* published in 1500.

The *Cortes* of Toledo in 1502 petitioned that the laws most used in the *fueros* be unified and the confusion cleared away. The Catholic Kings entrusted this task to Palacio Rubios. After the death of Doña Isabella, Don Ferdinand published these as the Laws of Toro in 1505. They were intended to be supplementary and explanatory of laws already in force and touch on matrimony, inheritance, entail, etc. These laws of Toro have been glossed many times: by Castillo, by Palacio Rubios, Gómez and others, increasing the confusion until in the edition of Medino del Campo of 1555, Miguel de Cifuentes has so swamped the text in commentaries that it is difficult to find it.

In the first law, the king is recognized as the final interpreter who in making his decisions is to follow as his authorities Bartolus, Baldo, Juan Andrés and Abad.

Further petitions to Don Charles V in 1523 to settle all disputes by a definitive compilation, did not bear fruit until the *Nova Recopilación* of Don Philip II. It is poorly arranged and contradictory. The king was designated final interpreter, and his decisions with the advice of the *Consejo Real* are known as *autos acordados.* These became incorporated into the code. The king relied on the Roman law to furnish him with the principles with which to interpret the mass of notes, additions and interpretations piled up in the previous two centuries. In 1743 Don Charles III ordered a supplement and Don Charles IV another in 1805. This produced the *Novíssima Recopilación de las leyes de España,* which has the merit of having everything possible in it, and if there was chaos before, this code does nothing to remove it.[80] In the *Novíssima Recopilación* is laid down the order in which the judges are to follow the various codes in their decisions: the *Recopilación, Fuero Real, Las Siete Partidas* and the authorities are still Bartolus, Juan Andrés and Abad.[81]

[80] *Los Códigos Españoles,* Vol. VII, p. ix.
[81] *Lib.* III, *Tít.* II, 1, 3.

Part II

ADMINISTRATIVE MACHINERY

Cives ideo vocati quod in unum coeuntes vivant, ut vita communis et ornatior fiat et tutior.

St. Isidore, Etymol., Lib. IX, c. 4

Legis conditor debet amare Deum et in ea condenda prae oculis eum habere ut sic perfecta et justa. Item debet justitiam et bonum commune diligere et scire bonum ab illicito separare nec pudeat eum si injusta sibi videatur, corrigere.

Partida Primera, Título I, l. 11

Nam regnum est quidam hortus, cuius arbores populus Rex domini horti et aqua qua rigatur, judices cultores proceres et milites custodes leges et iura vallum, judicium et justitia murus.

Partida Segunda, Título X, l. 2.

SAINT AUGUSTIN

Chapter V

The Kingship

THE administrative machinery of the Spanish government was embodied in the King and the Councils, the Municipalities and the *Cortes.*

In developing the institutions to carry out the theories of government which formed the normal material of their political thought, the Spanish were not as inept as might appear from a hasty survey. Their institutions aimed to be the media through which principles were applied to the concrete reality of the business of government. By the nature of the theory which never lost sight of the personal and the individual, the media could not be extended to embrace too wide a field. As the centralizing of Spanish political authority proceeded, and the various units of Spain were linked, or merged together, a serious conflict was introduced. The traditional institutions were based upon a theory of reciprocal rights and duties, that is of relationships, mutually arising out of the fact that those having such relationships acknowledged them in view of their common and final end, and not because of anything of value in themselves. Hence when they were brought face to face with a situation in which these relationships, particularly on the economic and political side, were found under the stress of this centralization and expansion, to be so complex as to appear to have a significance in themselves, a significance which eventually would demand a new theory, or at least a recasting of the old theory so as to provide for new institutions, the Spanish were unprepared.

Whether this problem was present to the thought of St. Thomas when he insisted that the state is a natural institution and the solution of the problems arising out of his more definite conception of the state, was supplied in the principles to be deduced from this, is a point that did not strike the Spanish of this period. The Spanish were the first people to have, in their conquests in the New World, a really wide framework for the conception of a state that had developed since St. Augustine stated his distinctively Christian-philosophical principles of government. It was unfortunate that the situation arose at a time when the Spanish tradition was being confused as a result of the introduction of the Roman law philosophy.

St. Augustine, however, did not evince in his writings any enthusiasm for large states. He seems to have preferred small groups,[1] though he did not take up the subject in detail. Could his great principle that the perfect man produces the perfect state, and good government results, when men have been made good, be realized in political entities like the Spanish possessions or modern states? Does not size reach a point beyond the power of human limitations to manage? Modern thought sees in the large state the greatest problem to be one of control. Having taken over the idea that the state is a natural institution, the moderns see in it only one end, which may be summed up in the word economics, just as justice under the influence of the Stoic ideas is being reduced to a mere means of receiving organization; that is, an arbitrary balancing of conflicting interests. Justice torn from its Divine source becomes nothing more than a function of the will, guided by reason, it is true, but

[1] Combès, op. cit., p. 89.

reason interpreted in the purely empirical sense of a synthesis of social experience. Tradition becomes but crystallized inertia.[2] The institutions of the modern state are reflecting this influence. Spanish institutions came to a crisis just when other countries, such as England and France, were going in for applied economics on the Stoic plan. They were not able to weather the storm and to provide for the permanence of the organization the Spanish had built up. Some reasons for this may be seen in a study of the development of their medieval institutions.

In the administrative machinery developed by Spain, the kingship was easily the most important, being the agency as it were to carry out justice, the aim of civil society. According to Eximeniç (d. 1416), one of the best writers on the science of government,[3] *regiment* or government was the authority and jurisdiction "given to the ruler to remove evil from the people willingly or by force, and to spur them on to good." This was the common traditional view, in Aragon as well as in Castile.

Two main ideas colored the concept of king, the first applied to the character the king should have and the second to the powers. St. Augustine formulated the norms for both and often his very words are used to describe them. In the early times of the Spanish state, stress was laid on the character; later after the Reconquest, in view of the greater complexity, the king began to assume powers and to make out of the kingship an institution not at first contemplated in theory.

In St. Augustine's view the king was to be a leader of public opinion, a center of national unity, a focus from

[2] Cf. Seillière, *La Philosophie de l'Impérialisme*, Paris, 1911; also Hauser, *La Nouvelle Orientation économique*, Paris, 1921.

[3] *Crestía é Llibre de regiment de Princeps é de la cosa publica*, 1379, dada al presidente per lunyarlos de mal per grat ó per forza é per promourelos a be.

which the national energies might radiate, a symbol of the collective mind of the people, but not the agent of their will in the modern sense. The people's will entered in only in regard to the choice of the one who could occupy the kingship, and as a force to set him aside in case he should violate the conditions on which he was given the power with authority.

As the first function of the king was to see that justice was secured to his people, the first obligation he was bound to keep in mind was that he, no less than his people, was subject to the law. The arguments for this are stated in the Forum Iudiciorum.[4] Since God Who is the most powerful King over all things, the Creator and sole Providence over the safety and welfare of all, enjoins upon all on earth the obligations to guard justice as set forth in the holy law, it befits each one however powerful he may be, to submit himself to the commandments. And further on it is stated, that as the king wishes to guard the commandments of God, he gives laws, jointly for himself and his subjects, who obey him, and for those who may come after him and the people who may be of his realm. No one, whatever power or dignity he may have, may be excused from keeping the laws.

The king was the head of his people, as the head is of the body,[5] defender of their life and of their safety, and he should guard their safety not only in word but also in deed, and have a care to what the people may ask.[6] No prince may constrain his subject by force, or remit the debt which one owes to another, because no one should side with injustice. In turn the prince should have what belongs to him, but it

[4] *Lib.* II, *Tít.* I, *ley* 2.
[5] *F.I., Lib.* II, *Tít.* I, *ley* 4.
[6] *F.I., Lib.* II, *Tít.* I, *ley* 5.

must be observed that before any prince may have the kingdom, he must promise by oath to keep the law.[7]

It is of interest to note that the title of this law—on taking away from princes the desire to dominate—is decidedly reminiscent of Augustine, as indeed are all the ideas in the passage. In discussing the attributes of power in a ruler, St. Augustine divides them under three headings, officium imperandi, officium providendi, officium consulendi. In discharging the duties of the first the ruler must avoid especially the passion to dominate and the pride of ruling; that is, he must not look upon his power to command as a personal possession, but as a necessary adjunct to his duty of guarding and directing the public welfare. His second duty (providendi) is to watch over the needs of his people, in short to become their providence. Thirdly, he should advise them, serve them, according to the precept that one should love one's neighbor as oneself.[8]

Because of these services and in view of the necessary cooperation from the people, rebels against the prince, or against the land, should be punished,[9] and the prince must be spoken of with respect.[10] The king was permitted the power of amending laws, but not with retroactive force.[11] The king also had power to name judges, in his general function of seeing that justice was done, and to define the commission of the judge,[12] and punishment was provided for

[7] See also *Las Siete Partidas, Partida Segunda, Tít.* I, *leyes* 2, 8.

[8] De Civ. Dei, xix, 14; for comments on this and ideas developed from it, see Combès, opus cit.

[9] *F.I., Lib.* II, *Tít.* I, *ley* 6; *Fuero Real, Lib.* I, *Tít.* II, *ley* 1; *Las Siete Partidas, Partida Segunda, Tít.* xiii, *leyes* 1, 6; *Partida quinta, Tít.* iv, *ley* 2; *Partida Sesenta, Tít.* II, *leyes* 1, 2, 4.

[10] *F.I., Lib.* II, *Tít.* I, *ley* 7; *Fuero Real, Lib.* I, *Tít.* II, *ley* 2; *Partida Segunda, Tít.* xiii, *leyes* 4, 7; *Partida Sesenta, Tít.* II, *leyes* 6, 13.

[11] *F.I., Lib.* II, *Tít.* I, *ley* 12. Suits once terminated under the old law, could not be reopened, but suits not yet concluded might be decided according to the new or amended law. See also *Partida Primera, Tít.* I, *ley* 14.

[12] *F.I., Lib.* II, *Tít.* I, *ley* 13, but the contestants might choose one to decide, or one be appointed by another judge. See also *Fuero Real, Lib.* I, *Tít.* VII, *ley* 2; *Partida Tercera, Tít.* iv, *leyes* 2, 17, 19, 20, 23; *F.I., Lib.* II, *Tít.* I, *ley* 15.

those judging without jurisdiction.[13] The king retained the final decision, in cases of complaint against unjust judges. The Bishops had the duty of admonishing and setting aside their judgments, but if the judges objected, the whole matter was to be submitted in writing to the king who would confirm or not the decision of the Bishop according as it seemed right.[14] The power of the king to give decisions was checked through another law, which held that a judgment made at the command of the king, or through fear, if it were unjust, was not valid.[15]

The conditions of the times during which the Forum Iudiciorum was codified, precluded any more formal delineations of the powers of the king. He was always recognized as the responsible head of the nation, however, and in the discharge of this office took on gradually more duties as the necessities of the times demanded, as may be seen from the history of the period.

In the thirteenth century, special circumstances contributed greatly to increase the personal prestige of the monarch as apart from the monarchy, both in Castile and Aragon. Characters such as Don Ferdinand III the Saint and Don Alfonso X of Castile, Don Jaime I the Conqueror and Don Pedro III the Great of Aragon, attached a brilliancy to the monarchy not soon to be forgotten; and the steady advance over the Moorish power and consequent reorganization necessary in the new territories, forced an initiative upon the kings greater than in the past.

This was the century also of expansion beyond Spain. The formation of new foreign policies represented by the desires of both the Castilian and Aragonese monarchs to play

[13] *F.I., Lib.* II, *Tit.* I, *ley* 16.

[14] *F.I., Lib.* II, *Tit.* I, *ley* 28. *Lib.* XII, *Tit.* I, *ley* 3, extends the powers of the Bishops, but it is lacking in the Latin text.

[15] *F.I., Lib.* II, *Tit.* I, *ley* 27. Also *Fuero Real, Lib.* I, *Tit.* XI, *levy* 4; *Partida Tercera, Tit.* xxii, *ley* 1, *Tit.* xxvi, *ley* 3.

a part in the affairs of France and Italy, in the Empire and in Africa, added prestige. This was the period of the universities, of the great deeds of the military orders, of the founding of the mendicant friars, of Scholasticism, of the great glossators and the study of the problems of government.

Don Ferdinand III is one of the glorious figures of the Reconquest, famous as a warrior against the Moors, a great administrator and a patron of learning. He carried Spanish arms to the gates of Granada, captured Córdova and Seville and was planning a crusade into Africa when he died. He united the Universities of Plasencia and Salamanca and his *fueros* to Córdova, Carmona, Tuy and Seville attest his administrative interests.

His son and successor, Don Alfonso X, became the inspiration of a splendid revival of Spanish culture, which earned for him the title of the Wise. His foreign policy, preoccupied with the thought of the imperial crown which was offered to him in 1257, widened the horizon of Castilian interests into Navarre, France and Italy. The dissensions over the succession between the partisans of Don Sancho IV and Don Ferdinand de la Cerda, though disastrous for the unity of his kingdom, was not without its lessons for the students of the codes. Learning received his special devotion. He favored the University of Salamanca, established at Seville a school for the study of Latin and Arabic and another at Toledo for the study of Hebrew and Arabic, which resulted in many valuable translations. One influence of this encouragement of learning may be noted in the Summulae Logicales (based on the Logic of Aristotle and Porfirio), written by Petrus Hispanus (1226-77), who was born in Spain but died as Pope John XXI.

Spanish was beginning to supplant Latin as the official and literary language. Don Ferdinand III's order to translate the Forum Iudiciorum into Spanish gave impetus to this, as did also Don Alfonso's efforts to have written the *Estoria de Espanna* and the *Grande e General Estoria* (still in manuscript). Among the works on government of this period are: the *Libro de los conseios et conseieros de los principes para su buen gobierno* of Pedro Gómez Barroso, friend of Don Sancho IV. In the fourteenth century, Fray Johan García de Castro Xerez, at the order of Bernard Bishop of Osma, translated the de Regimine of Egidio Colonna, known in Spain as *El regimiento de principes*, for the instruction of the young prince who was later to ascend the throne as Don Pedro I. The great Castilian jurists of this age were: Jácome Ruiz, author of *Las Flores de las Leyes*, and the *Doctrinal de los pleitos*; Fernando Martínez who wrote *Margarita de los pleitos*; Bernardo Compostelano who wrote commentaries on the Digests and Decretals and a Breviarium iuris canonici; the canonist John of God who wrote Cavillationes seu doctrina advocatorum partium et assensorum; the famous glossators of the Decretals, Vicente Hispano and Juan García.

In the fourteenth century, Don Gonzalez de Bustamente, Bishop of Segovia, wrote a repertory of canon law, and Don Vicente Arias de Balboa, Bishop of Plasencia, wrote a gloss on the *Fuero Real* and a commentary on the *Ordenamiento de Alcalá*, while in the following century lived Juan Alfonso de Benevente, the great professor of Canon Law. Don Sancho IV founded the College of Alcalá in 1293, and both he and his father were generous patrons of libraries. Don Alfonso X gave many books to the Monasteries of Albelda and Nájera. Among other famous libraries were those of Don Gonzalo Palomeque at Cuenca, and of Don Pedro López de Ayala, Don Enrique de Villena, the Marquis of Santillana, the Count of Haro, and Don Juan Nuñez de Guzmán, Master of Calatrava, all in the fifteenth century. Earlier the library of the Archbishop of Toledo, Don Gil de Albornoz, and of that in San Miguel in Santiago were famous.

A similar story may be told of Aragon. With the reign of Don Jaime I the Conqueror (he began to rule in 1218), a new era arose in the eastern kingdoms. Having conquered Valencia and the Balearic Islands, he was not able to advance further on the mainland because of the Castilian occupation of Murcia. Aragonese policy then turned to the problem of the Mediterranean and affairs in Italy. Don Jaime's character, decisive, intrepid, adventurous, ambitious, indifferent somewhat to the means of accomplishing his ends, made him remarkable in an age when energy and courage were common characteristics and contributed in no slight degree to his success in dominating his nobles. His successor, Don Pedro III the Great, was led to take an active part in Italian politics through his marriage with Doña Constanza, descended from the Emperor Frederick II through her father Manfred, who had been defeated by Charles of Anjou, King of Naples. The tyrannical rule of Charles produced such discontent that two of the leading nobles approached Don Pedro for aid. As his queen, heiress of the Suabian family, was the only one who could produce legitimate title to the throne of the Two Sicilies, Don Pedro was ready to enter into an agreement to defend her rights against Charles of Anjou. He succeeded in his campaigns, was crowned King of the Two Sicilies at Palermo in 1282 and his arms spread terror throughout Sicily. This drew down on his head the disapproval of Pope Martin IV, who excommunicated him and placed his kingdom under an interdict. The Aragonese looked with no favorable eyes on these acts of their king and in the famous *Unión* attempted to bring him to a sense of his position in Aragon, and to remind him of the ancient *fueros* and customs, which he was tending to contravene by his Roman law ideas. The struggle carried into the succeeding reigns tended to strengthen the traditional conception of the status of the monarchy, but also to favor the spread of the Justinian principles which received added prestige from the foreign policies adopted.

At this time Andronicus Paleologus, ruler of Constantinople, was recruiting his forces in Sicily for an attack on the Osmanli Turks. Some of the light armed militia of Don Fadrique son of Don Pedro III, joined the Greek forces under Don Berenguer de Entenza and Don Fernando Ahonés and distinguished themselves in Asia Minor with such effect that as a result a chain of strategic positions in the Near East was held for the Aragonese and Catalans which secured for the Crown of Aragon the maritime hegemony of the Mediterranean in the fourteenth century.[16] Don Alfonso IV of Aragon confirmed the celebrated Statute of Don Jaime II by which the Kingdoms of Aragon, Valencia and the Principality of Cataluña were united under the Crown of Aragon. Each was autonomous but under the jurisdiction of the King of Aragon.[17]

Culture was fostered in the eastern kingdoms no less than in Castile, though the universities appeared somewhat later. The Royal and Pontifical University of Lérida was founded by Don Jaime II in 1300,[18] the University of Huesca by Don Pedro IV in 1354, Perpigñán in 1350, Barcelona, 1450, Saragossa, 1474. In Mallorca there were special schools devoted to the study of oriental languages. Students from all

[16] Consult the works of Antonio Rubió y Lluch, such as *La lengua y la cultura catalana en Grecia en el siglo XIV, Catalunya a Grecia. Estudios históricos i literaris,* Barcelona, 1906.

[17] *Vos senyor sots ab sobirana cura e vigilancia, entendre en la publica utilitat, de manera que en aquella sien fetes obres bones e virtuoses e della expella des totes maler e vicioses, con los principeps e senyors del mon sien presos per Deu en lurs senyories a repos de cor ne de cors, ans a gran ansia e treball si perfectamente volen exercir lurs officis, Cortes* of Perpignan, 1410.

[18] Lérida was a rich, flourishing city with Roman traditions. It was the first city to edit its customary legislation (Consuetudines Ilerdenses, of Guillermo Botet, 1227) and remained independent of Cataluña until the twelfth century.

these went to Paris, Toulouse, Rome, Bologna, Oxford and Germany for further studies. The jurists in particular attended Bologna, notably Ramón de Peñafort, Vidal de Cañellas, Pedro Albert and Arnaldo de Gurb.

Among the best known writers on government of this period are: Pere Torella, who compiled *Le Libre de les franqueses e dels privilegis de Mallorca e dels Usatges de Barcelona;* Arnau Estanyol who translated the *Regiment de princeps* of Egidio Romano, R. de Presles who translated into Catalán St. Augustine's City of God, and the most famous of all, Eximeniç, who wrote the *Regiment de la cosa publica.*

The Aragonese *fueros* were compiled at the order of Don Jaime I under the direction of Don Vidal de Cañellas which was approved by the *Cortes* of Huesca in 1247. The influence of the Justinian studies is marked in this. De Cañellas also edited the *fueros* of Valencia. The *fueros* of Saragossa (1300) were translated into Latin by the *Justicia* Jimén Pérez de Salanova and with the laws approved in the *Cortes* of 1301 and 1367 were put into Latin by the Justicias Juan López de Sese and Domingo Cerdán. The compilation of Huesca of the fifteenth century contains some of the *fueros* translated by Cerdán.

Cataluña was the country of the jurists from Guillermo de ça Sala and Guillermo Botet of Lérida to Jaime Montjuich, Ramón Ballester, Jaime Cardó, Berenguer Vives and Pere Beçet all of the fourteenth century. In the fifteenth century the most famous jurist is Jaime Callís (Jacobo Calicio) of Vich who wrote Extravagatorium Curiarum, Directorum pacis et treuge, Super Usaticos Catholoniae elucidarium soni emisi. The great counsellor of Don Alfonso V, Don Tomás Mieres, wrote an important work, Apparatus aurei super constitutionibus et capitulis Curiarum generalium Catholoniae, and Pedro Belluga wrote his Speculum principum in 1440, the first positive scientific treatment of law. It was printed in Paris, 1530 and Brussels in 1655. The Valencian legislation was compiled in 1239 by Vidal de Cañellas.[19]

Very few of these have been studied by modern writers and of all these works the most easily available to students in the United States is *Las Siete Partidas.* These others are based upon the same tradition and hence a study of the second *Partida* will give a fair idea of how the institution of kingship had been shaping up during the centuries.

From the prologue to this *Partida,* we learn that the royal power is now looked upon as the temporal power, coördinate with the spiritual. "There are two swords by which the world is maintained." The spiritual deals with the hidden, the temporal with open evils.[20] On the principles of right reason, the two powers are always in accord and each is to aid the other. For them to disagree in violation of the commandment of God would end the conditions of peace.[21] Moreover, sovereignty and kingship coincide. The second law of the first Title of this *Partida* takes up the question of the powers inhering in sovereignty. The first attribute is the power of granting new laws or *fueros,* and if the public safety demanded it, to change or interpret an old law; to introduce a new custom, to abrogate one which might be disadvantageous. This power belongs to the emperor or king, de iure, and to none other save by grant of the emperor.

He may grant new market concessions, impose tolls, coin money, divide provinces and fix the boundaries of cities and towns, declare war, make truces, interpret doubtful privileges either by himself or with other judges in consultation, create

[19] Ballesteros, III, pp. 171-213, 423-32, 580-99.

[20] St. Augustine, Brev. collationis in P.L. xliii, 652.

[21] López gives many authorities for his comment, notably the De Regimine, of St. Thomas, c. 18, 19. Cf. also Combès, op. cit., pp. 306 sq.—the state rules the exterior life, the Church the interior, Brev. collationis, 16, in P.L. xliii, 652.

judges, exact tribute from the subject according to ancient usages, provided it be not used for evil purposes. He may not impose any tribute upon his subject, unless by consent of the subject, or as penalty for a crime, but if he should receive it in view of the necessity of the state for the common utility of the land, when given under such condition, the title over it should result from a fair exchange or for a greater price by the free will of the good men (boni viri). This power goes immediately to the emperor because his election is made by the choice of the empire, or the greater part.[22] The powers were by no means absolute and the rights of the people were protected.

De facto; the emperor could punish and restrain those who do not obey him; maintain arms and fortresses within the limits of his territories and reward his servitors. But he was enjoined to seek the aid of wise and prudent counsellors and keep in mind that he could claim power as long as he was just, merciful, respecting the people in word and in deed. To despise and to treat his subjects with contempt and injustice, would lose him the love of his subjects. Nor should he contemplate war without much counsel.[23]

An interesting light is thrown on the Spanish conception of the kingship in the thirteenth law of the thirteenth Title of this *Partida.* The gloss makes the point that the people should know the king in his essence, in the Aristotelian sense of knowing things through their causes. That is they should see in him their temporal lord, who in the name of God has authority over them. Secondly, they should know him through his effects, that is in his works, since he is put over

[22] *Partida Segunda, Tít.* I, *ley* 2.

[23] Ibid., *leyes* 3, 4. *Leyes* 5-8 discuss the powers of the king on the same plan. *Ley* 9 takes up the question of the king's title. Four titles are recognized: succession, direct or nearest in descent; heirs lacking, by election, according to the law of nations; marriage, i.e., the queen's consort had the title of king but no jurisdiction. Opinions were divided on this, but in the case of the Catholic Kings, Ferdinand had no jurisdiction outside of his own realms, though Isabella made a point of consulting him. The fourth title was by grant of Pope or Emperor.

them to do justice, to give each one his rights, to defend them.[24]

The monarchy could never be considered as a mere creature of the will of the people, invested as it was with this sacred character of authority. Whatever share the people might have in what the moderns would call the government, was certainly never one in which they could be considered as having the right to participate directly in its functions. Those who would criticize the Spanish for not developing the *Cortes* into a legislative body, such as the American Congress, or such absolute arbiters of national destiny as the French or English Parliaments, fail utterly to grasp what the Spanish idea was. The people were a collection of men in one mystical body and as such were to be loved, honored and guarded by the king, and any action he should take in their regard, was to be directed from the point of view of protecting their rights and in no sense of infringing on them.[25]

De Vitoria summed up and reflected the best opinions of the sixteenth century view of sovereignty. In discussing the origins and end of civil society he refutes those who would consider the one who held civil power as having a mere mandate of the people, and denies that the civil power is the sum of the rights which may have been transmitted through the members of civil society when constituted, and upholds the theory of the unity of the civil power against those who

[24] The text of this law is lacking in the edition used in this essay.

[25] *Partida Segunda, Tít.* X, *ley* 1: Populus est hominum mediocrium majorum mediocrium et minorum adunatio. Lopez gives as his authorities Balduino (L. Etiam col. 5, c. de execut. rei jud.), Bartolus (L. I, ff. ad municip. abb. c.1 de Vita et honestat. cleric.) and quotes Isidore, Cives ideo vocati quod in unum coeuntes vivant, ut vita communis et ornatior fiat et tutior, Etymol., Lib. IX, c.4.

Nam regnum est quidem hortus, cuius arbores populus. Rex domini horti et aqua qua rigatur judices cultores proceres et milites custodes, leges et iura vallum, judicum et justicia murus, *Partida Segunda, Tít.* X, *ley* 2 (For the kingdom is like a garden, of which the people are the trees. The king is the lord of the garden and it is watered with water with which the judges and leading men cultivate it, laws and rights are its ramparts, soldiers its guards, judgment and justice its wall). *F.I., Lib.* I, *Tít.* I, *ley* 8.

oppose the power of the republic or of the people to that of the chief of state.[26]

For such an exalted office it was recognized that an equally exalted character was necessary to fill it suitably. Rules were laid down for the formation of such a character, and in Titles II-IX of the second *Partida* are discussed the principles upon which a king should form himself. He must first know, love and fear God, for to govern in justice and right reason the aid of God is necessary.[27] And as a man is what he thinks in his heart, the king should not be ambitious to dominate, to possess great riches, to be vicious.[28] His words should be few and well chosen and careful.[29] In his works he should be temperate and pure, his dress proper, his manners courteous; always he should be self-controlled, guarding against ambition to dominate.[30] His education should be provided for, and he should acquire a knowledge of men.[31] Titles VI-IX remind him of his duties and bearing towards his wife, family, parents and officials of the court.

All this in the stately Latin of the time catches up the great principles of Christian morality so eloquently portrayed by St. Augustine,[32] and is a very striking example of how deeply his thought and his expression had penetrated the Spanish mind. Though in practice, many Spanish kings might fall below this ideal, in theory none ever paid allegiance to anything less, and there were never lacking subjects to remind the king of his deficiencies and recall him to his duties. In the interpretation of these duties, the king was left

[26] Hinojosa, E de, *Estudios sobre la Historia del derecho español*, article *Francisco de Vitoria*, p. 221.
[27] *Tít.* II.
[28] *Tít.* III.
[29] *Tít.* IV.
[30] *Tít.* V, especially *leyes* 9-15.
[31] Ibid., *leyes* 16, 17.
[32] Combès, op. cit., p. 113, where he summarizes from the De Civitate Dei (v, 24), Augustine's idea of a Christian prince, who brings about the rule of justice, fears, loves and adores God, prefers spiritual kingdoms to royalty, slow to punish, prompt to pardon, and punishes only for the well-being of the state, and who prefers to command his passions rather than the peoples of the earth.

to the guidance of his conscience, but not in a purely subjective sense. As a Catholic he had at hand for direction and advice, the Sacrament of Penance, and the King's confessor was always considered one of the most important officials of the court.[33] This explains why the royal confessor was given a seat in the important councils (as they were established) in which questions were discussed that later might become matter for the king's conscience, so that he would be in the best possible situation to give wise and prudent advice; and not as so many non-Catholic writers assume because the Church wished to dominate the state. These writers fail to see the point of view of the Catholic, though many admit that until the eighteenth century at least the majority of the Catholic kings took their duties seriously and to the best of their ability directed their actions as their consciences dictated. As St. Augustine and others have remarked, perfection is not to be found on earth.

If these were the lines on which the king was expected to proceed, his people in their turn should know, love and serve God by reason and by faith,[34] be desirous always for the good of the king; they should have a care for his good reputation but should speak the truth of him and not flatter him; they should serve him in the fear that is born of love and results in obedience, nor should they rise up against him.[35]

Not that the people were expected to accept the king's injustices or usurpations in patient silence. The Spanish mind was as clear on the subject of a tyrant as was the Christian medieval mind generally, and in a separate law defined this term.[36] "One is called a tyrant who by force or treach-

---

[33] *Partida Segunda, Tít.* IX, *ley* 3, defining the king's confessor as chaplain of the court, and one of the most honored officials. See also *F.I., Lib.* II, *Tít.* 1, *ley* 29, censor regis, a magistrate of the court.

[34] *Partida Segunda, Tít.* XII.

[35] Ibid., *Tít.* XIII, *leyes* 1, 2, 3, 4, 5, 6 (which recalls *F.I., Primo Titulo, ley* 9; *Lib.* II, *Tít.* I, *ley* 6), 7, 8, 9, 10, 11, 12, 13, 14, 15.

[36] Ibid., *Tít.* I, *ley* 10.

ery takes possession of the kingdom," and the foundation of his tyranny is that he seeks his own advantage and not the common good. Tyrants are always afraid of losing their kingdom, and in their tyrannizing use a triple art, first to keep their subjects ignorant, second to sow seeds of discord, and third to keep them poor and busy at many things so that they have no time to think or plot against him.[37]

May one kill a tyrant? The common opinion seemed to be that he could be disposed of,[38] at least if the following from the literature may be taken as a guide to public opinion. Guillén de Castro in *Las Hazañas del Cid*,[39] writes:

> *Arias: Llevad preso ese traido.*
> *Bellido: ¿Traición es poner la mano en un rey que fué tirano?*
> *Gonzalo: Nunca es tirano el señor.*[40]

and in *Amor* constante says:

> *Rey: ¿y es razón que muera un rey?*
> *Nisida: Si es tirano.*
> *un Grande: Siendo rey, esté en su mano*
> *Cuanto quisiere hacer*
> *Olio: El rey en siendo hacer*
> *Luego lo deja de ser.*[41]

---

[37] Cf. St. Gregory 12 Lib. Moratorium, c. 18; Bartolus, Tract. De Tyrannia, adds who wishes to take by force a principality.

[38] De Regimine, Lib. I, c. vi. Note the conditions.

[39] This famous play forms the second part of the *Mocedades del Cid*, and deals with the dramatic incidents connected with the murder of Don Sancho by the insignificant Bellido de Olfos. Don Ferdinand had divided his kingdom among his children leaving to his daughter, Doña Urraca, Zamora, and warning Sancho that if he disobeyed his wishes and attempted to take more than his share, his curse would fall upon him. Don Sancho disregarded the warning and proceeded to attack his brothers and to besiege Zamora. The play recounts the events leading up to the tragic murder of Don Sancho, and in the course of the action many references are made to the popular traditions on the monarchy.

[40] Arias: Lead away this traitor.
Bellido: Is it treason to put hand upon a king who is tyrannical?
Gonzalo: Never is a traitor, the lord.

[41] Rey: Is it right that a king should die?
Noble: Being king he has the power to do as he wishes.
A Noble: Being king he has the power to do as he wishes.
Olio: The king doing such, then fails to be such.

It is interesting to note that it is the noble who favors the absolute power.

Lope de Vega in *La Estrella de Seville* sets down the following opinion:

Pues ¿qué debo obedecer?
La ley que fuese primero
Mas no hay ley qué á aquesto oblique,
Mas si hay: que aunque injuste el Rey
Es obedecerle ley,
A él despues Dios le castigue.[42]

Calderón in *El Alcalde de Zalamer*, in his use of the word *honor* throws a vivid light on the attitude to the king. *Honor* has much more than the significance of the English honor; it is an all embracing term which includes all that becomes a man, his inalienable rights and his inviolable dignity resulting from his eternal destiny.

Al rey la hacienda y la vida
Se ha de dar: pero el honor
Es patrimonio del alma
y el Alma sólo es de Dios.[43]

The popular tradition on the responsibility of the king to the people may be seen in this quotation from the *Regimiento de Principes* of Gómez Manrique, part of an address to Doña Isabella the Catholic:

Ca no vos demandarán
Cuenta de los que rezays
Non si vos disciplinays
Non vos lo preguntaran. . . .

[42] Then whom ought I to obey?
The law which should be first,
But there is no law which obliges to that,
But if there were, that however unjust the king
The law is to obey him,
May God punish him then.

[43] To the king fortune and life
Must be given; but honor
Is the patrimony of the soul
And the soul belongs to God alone.

Si los culpados punistes
O los malos consentistes
desto sera la quistion [44]

And if we glance through even a small portion of the voluminous literature discussing government and the powers of the king, it is very evident that the normal Spanish view was always that of the earlier tradition,—the king is entrusted with the administration of justice by God,[45] he is the guardian and protector of his people and in no sense do they have to tolerate either injustice or tyranny.

The following from Pedro Simón Abril sums this up where he comments on the Republic of Plato: [46] "What may be inferred for the good ruling of a kingdom is that neither the king nor those who rule for him, have absolute power in such a manner that their will may have to be taken for law. Because the law must be the rule with which justice has to be regulated and the rule, if it is to be a rule, must be just, and not to be twisted to mean one thing at one time and something different at another. This is not left free to the will of man, since it is so changeable and so subject to the passions that deflect it." Further on he adds that the king is the protector and guarantor of the laws, he must put them into execution. He may make laws on two conditions, that they be beneficial to all, not only for some, be freely accepted, for when force enters, liberty ceases.

The famous Sor María de Jesus de Agreda in various letters to Don Philip IV, holds that the king governs in participation

[44] They will not ask of you
Account of the things which you beg,
Not if you instruct them,
No they will not ask you this,
Or of you punish the guilty,
But if you consent to evils,
Then will come the question.

[45] Note the phrase of Juan Martínez, writing in the latter part of the reign of Don Juan II, *Como por Dios la alta justicia, al rey de la tierra es encomendada.*

[46] He was born in 1530 in Alcaráz, and for twenty-four years was professor of humanities at the University of Saragossa. See Becker, Jerónimo, *La Tradición política española,* Madrid, 1896, to whom I am indebted for many of the quotations.

with God, and is obligated to fulfill and realize in the world, justice, in order to realize the ends of Providence on earth. She defends the duty of respecting and fulfilling the will of the people, in so far as it accords with justice. Fray Marco Antonio de Camor,[47] though he conceded to the king the power to make laws, held that the king as well as his subjects were bound by the natural law, and the people were not for the government but the government was for the people. The change in the point of view of the sixteenth century in regard to the tradition is shown in the following selections. The Franciscan, Alfonso de Castro (1495-1558), who assisted at the Council of Trent and went with Don Philip II to the Low Countries, held that by the natural law it belongs to the people to make laws: the king is given for the use of the people, not the people for the use of the king; and that king who exceeds his authority, publishing laws without considering the usage and customs of the country, is a tyrant.[48] Diego Covarrubias y Leiva (1512-77), called the Spanish Bartolus, defined the power of the republic as superior to that of the king; the royal power was established by free election of the people, nor could the king abuse it without being a tyrant.[49] Bartolomé Felippe,[50] Furio Ceriol,[51] Domingo de Soto,[52] Fox Morcillo,[53] Luis de Molina,[54] and Suarez,[55] all hold that the king must guard the laws, obey them, and if he commands anything unjust

---

47 Published in 1592 at Barcelona, *Microsomia y Gobierno del hombre cristiano.*

48 De potestate legis poenalia, Salamanca, 1551.

49 His great work is Practicarum quaestionum, Lugdani, 1594. He taught law at Salamanca and Oviedo, was Bishop of Segovia, distinguished himself at Trent, and was a member of the Council of State.

50 Published at Coimbra, 1584, *Tractado del Consejo y de los consejeros de los principes.*

51 *Del consejo y consejeros del principe*, 1559.

52 De Iustitia et iure, 1556.

53 De Regni regisque institutione, 1556.

54 De Iustitia et iure, Cuenca, 1592, in six volumes. He considers the origin of royal power to be in the pact between the republic and the prince; once granted the king had the authority but failing to observe his contract, he could be put out.

55 De legibus ac de Deo legislatore, Coimbra, 1612.

or contrary to what God has commanded, no obedience is due him. The king must govern in accordance with the wishes and desires of the people, considering their welfare.[56] All would heartily concur in this saying from Raymond Lully:[57] The justice of the king is the peace of the people. More beautiful is the justice of the king than his crown. The bad prince and the great demon should keep company.

So much for the ideal and theory of the king's character and authority. As an institution just what did the kingship imply? Was it a power of the government, or a branch of the government as we should say today? So some think who speak of the king as one of the coördinate arms of the government, along with the clergy, the nobility, the burgesses. Or did it comprise the whole government, these estates being but the expression of what we call today class interests, using this term as describing the different kinds of organizations which the social and economic necessities of man demand? Perhaps organization is too precise a word to use, as the various interests or relations, aside from the Church, had scarcely got beyond the stage of being a channel giving expression to the interest in question. The reasons for this are to be found partly in the long wars of the Reconquest and the special conditions created by the clash of two opposing cultures, and partly in the Augustinian theory. Research on the subject of Spanish medieval institutions and how they worked has not gone very far as yet, though what study has been made on the *Cortes* and the Municipalities throw some light on this subject. Whether these institutions would have developed into coördinate political departments on the basis of the division of the powers of government, placing them on an equality with the kingship, it is hard

[56] There are some differences among these authors as to whether the authority comes from God to the king directly or indirectly through the people, De Soto and Suarez in particular holding the latter view.

[57] He was born in 1235. From his *Arbol de la ciencia.*

to say in the present state of research. The normal lines of Spanish political development were deflected by the Roman law philosophy.

Discussions on the civil power as apart from the king's power, were going on during the sixteenth and seventeenth centuries, as may be gathered from some of the above quotations. The question of the origin of the king's power, whether directly from God, or indirectly from the people; of the part the people should have in the actual work of the government; of the relations between the civil power and the ecclesiastical with their respective jurisdictions—were debated then with as much learning as intensity of feeling. But again it is idle to speculate what modifications these ideas might have produced in the institutions.

This much it seems safe to say, that all during the troubled times of the Reconquest with the ups and downs varying between good and bad kings, the Spanish remained faithful to the fundamental conception that the government was embodied in the king and the government was one. The noblest and the loftiest expression of the later Spanish kingship is undoubtedly to be found in the regency of Cardinal Ximénez de Cisneros. His austerity and restraint, his wisdom and his keen penetration into the essences of the problems with which he was confronted, his firmness, his decisive authority, his grasp of the realities of justice, make him the greatest exemplar of the Spanish ideal ruler. As one of his biographers has described him, he was "*castellano por nacimiento, castellano por convicción, castellano por los procedimientos y español por lo uno y por lo otro y por todo*", the ideal which brought him close to the picture set forth in the De Regimine.[58] His ideals, says the same biographer, are at root

[58] Castilian by birth, Castilian in conviction, Castilian in procedure, Spanish in each and all. Conde de Cedillo, *El Cardenal Cisneros*, Madrid, 1921, p. 382. Cf. De regimine, Lib. IV, c. 15.

those sustained by St. Thomas, those found in the great national codes of the Forum Iudiciorum and *Las Siete Partidas,* those found so eloquently defended by the classical writers on public law of the golden century, as for example P. Rivadeneyra in his *Principe cristiano,* P. Mariana in his De Rege, Fray Juan Marquéz in his *Gobernador cristiano,* Fray Juan de Santa María in his *Tratado de republica y policia cristiana para Reyes y principes,* of Quevedo in his *Política de Dios gobierno de Cristo,* of Saavedra Fajardo in his *Empresas políticas.* The doctrine is all the same: all power and all authority comes from God, the Supreme Sovereign, and it is this principle which is the life of the Christian monarchy.[59]

The king was the monarchy and the monarchy was the king. If in working this out in concrete actions and practical details, the great Cardinal appeared more absolute in his conception of the monarchy than would be one who held to the limited monarchy suggested by St. Thomas Aquinas, it was not so much because his theory varied from that of St. Thomas, as that the necessities of his times forced him to place the emphasis on authority, rather than on what is called democracy. With him, the civil power, while strictly delimited from the ecclesiastical, was indissolubly entwined with the monarchy, and monarchy could only be an empty expression if it were not accompanied by all the prestige, force and authority necessary to impose its sovereignty.[60] It was not only because Cardinal Cisneros had vitally in mind the weakness and humiliations of Don Enrique IV and the disorderly nobility of the early fifteenth century and hence wished to reëstablish the prestige of government, but because he realized that the people and the nobility, the nerve,

[59] *El Cardenal Cisneros,* pp. 307-8.
[60] Ibid., p. 310.

flesh and blood of the state, would be helpless to the point of anarchy unless the monarchy should take upon itself their direction and guidance. This was the exclusive function of the monarchy and the whole machinery of government. In the following phrase he but reiterates the thoroughly Spanish idea: *"El bien de los subditos aun es ver syempre a los principes poderosos y que administren justicia, y con esto se rremedia todo por mano de Dios."* (The well being of the subject requires always powerful princes, that they may administer justice, and with this all will be remedied by the hand of God.[61]) And he would have agreed with Quevedo, "The king who governs himself, the king who helps himself by his own aid, who guards himself and watches over himself, is the one who will watch over his realms." [62]

Cardinal Cisneros may be said to have crystallized the conception of the Christian monarchy of the late Middle Ages. He has been called a dictator, but he always controlled his actions by the principles of the most ancient code of his people, as may be seen from this quotation from a letter to Don Diego López de Ayala of October 14, 1516: "I am certain that I have had to say or do nothing but what is comportable with the service of His Majesty and first with that of God, and with the welfare and peace of these realms." This was his norm of conduct, homage to the king as temporal representative of God and as distributor of justice for his people.

He did not hold that the people could intervene in the affairs of state with any efficacy, for he did not see the necessity of this. The government was for the well-being of the people and this could be secured without their intervention in affairs of state, for he considered them still an

---

[61] *Cartas del Cardenal*, p. 147.
[62] *Política de Dios gobierno de Cristo*, 1st part, c. v.

amorphous mass. With what care he could consider their welfare, may be seen from his administrative reforms and policies, and not the least in the instructions sent to the Hieronymite Fathers for their guidance in the affairs of Hispaniola in 1516.[63]

The monarchy as an institution under Cardinal Cisneros was indeed a collection of institutions. In the performance of the duties of the administrator of the common good, it took upon itself all the functions which could benefit the life of the people, the foundation of schools, academies and convents, the military defense against dangers from without and from within, the organization of the finances, the initiation of new economic policies in accordance with the needs of the kingdom, the creation of a foreign policy that would work for peace and not for war, the guardian of civilization and the prudent direction of its extension into barbarous regions. If it be objected that it needed a superman like the Cardinal to hold fast and true the threads of all these activities, and that the monarchy as an institution broke down under their weight, it cannot be denied that the conception of government permeating it was on a plane of ideals and principles unknown to any of the modern states. It was never intended that this institution was to have anything of the character of absolute government in the imperialistic connotation of the word.

[63] *Colecc. de Doc. inéd. relativo al descub . . .* 2nd series, Vol. IX, 1895, pp. 53-74.

SPANISH KING

Chapter VI

The Councils of the King

FROM the earliest codes it was recognized that in the discharge of such varied functions, the king would need advice and aid. While the final responsibility was his, he was cautioned in many a law [1] to ask for the advice of the best men available in his kingdom before undertaking new policies or making important decisions. Government was considered a specialized thing and required the trained specialist and more than one. This idea was not of course invented by the medieval Spaniard. The best Greek thought and Roman practice alike saw no room for the amateur in such weighty affairs. St. Augustine, in defining the character of the Christian prince, did not omit to notice the necessity of an *élite* of magistrates to collaborate with him, and in an interesting passage outlines their character with a fine sense of the dignity and high importance of public service.[2] It was from among such that the king was to seek his advisers and members of his councils.

Early in Spanish history the kings had councils of an advisory nature, or to relieve them of some of the duties of their charge, but their origins and exact functions are much debated by historians. The general opinion is that the Visigothic kings copied the Roman practice which they had observed in Italy. Theodoric, in the fifth century, noted the

[1] Law is used here in the medieval sense of a principle of action.
[2] Combès, op. cit., p. 116, quoting from De Ordine, II, 20, 54 in *P. L.*, vol. xxxii.

high Roman functionaries, invested with military, administrative and judicial powers. These were called comites and there were associated with them Gothic nobles called comes Gothorum.[3] The Gothic kings adopted this plan as they adopted so many of the Roman customs. While following the Roman view of monarchy,[4] they were accustomed to hold assemblies in which the various elements of their society were represented, the nobili viri, electores provinciales, sacerdotes, venerabiles episcopi, but these assemblies fell into abeyance during the struggles and assassinations which distinguished the successive reigns from Amalaric to Leovigild. The latter did not reëstablish them, though he revived the officio palatino.[5]

The officio palatino was created in imitation of the Senatus domesticus of Hadrian. It was composed of dukes, counts, governors of provinces, and constituted a kind of aula regia. It gave advice on affairs of state, accompanied the king and formed a supreme tribunal, says Colmeiro.[6] These officials had little power, but in the Eighth Council of Toledo, convoked by Recceswinth, it was decided that the king should be elected by the great ones of the nation chosen from among the palatine officials.[7] In the succeeding councils the king named those whom he wished to attend.[8] In the officio palatino the fiscals served; they could not be relieved from duty without a rescript from the king and their slaves and land were the property of the Crown.[9] Slaves could serve as fiscals

[3] Torréanaz, Conde de, *Los Consejos del Rey durante la Edad Media,* Madrid, 1884, I, pp. 51-2.

[4] Pérez-Pujol, op. cit., II, pp. 162-3.

[5] Ibid., p. 168.

[6] *El Poder Civil,* Madrid, 1885-6, I, pp. 97-8.

[7] Vos etiam illustres quos ex officio palatino huic sanctae synodo interesse mos primaevus obtinuit.

[8] Et vos illustres aulae regiae viros interesse huic sancto concilio delegit nostra sublimitas, XII Tolet.

Hoc solum vos honorabiles Dei sacerdotes cunctosque illustres aulae regiae seniores quos in hoc concilio nostrae serenitatis praeceptio, XVI Tolet.

Etiam vos illustre aulae regiae decus ac magnificorum virorum numerosus conventus quod huic honorabili coetui nostra interesse celsitudo praecepit, XVII Tolet.

[9] Cf. *F.I., Lib.* V, *Tít.* vii, *leyes* 15, 16; *Lib.* X, *Tít.* ii, *ley* 4.

by permission of the king, though there was strong objection to this in the Thirteenth Council of Toledo.[10] This council appears an exalted body with a membership made up from the clergy, military and nobles, to which were also admitted men of the lower classes.[11] Wamba gave the officio palatino judicial functions when he sentenced the seditious Paulus.[12] The king was obliged to seek the advice of the great men of his kingdom before deciding certain cases or granting pardon. The palatines and high ecclesiastics had guarantees that they could not be deprived of their dignities or possessions without the accusation against them being publicly debated.

The kings of the Reconquest continued the Gothic custom of holding councils. Don Alfonso the Chaste summoned to Oviedo, where he established his court, assemblies or councils for deliberation or advice on numerous affairs and his successors did the same at Oviedo, León or Coyanza. These were known under the titles of concilium, colloquium, curia or conventus. In these the officio palatino continued as assistant to the Crown in its executive functions, and began to take on the character of a permanent royal commission in the midst of the national assemblies, a high tribunal of justice and a permanent council for the chief of state.[13]

Those who were regularly called to attend the councils in the early Middle Ages were the comes or counts, direct descendants of the high functionaries who under this title assisted in the aula regia of the Visigothic kings. In the days of Don Alfonso I, the comes whether palatine officials or administrative officials representing the king in the Marches

[10] In dominorum suorum vehementius grassaverunt . . . in qua obscena servitutis conditio . . . ac proinde hortante pariter ac jubente praedicto gloriosissimo principe, hoc nostri coetus agregatio observandum instituit ut exceptis servis vel libertis fiscalibus, nullus servorum atque etiam libertorum quorum libet deinceps ad palatinum quando que transire permittatur officium.

[11] Torréanaz, op. cit., p. 68.

[12] Coniuro te per nomen omnipotentis Dei ut in hoc conventu fratrum meorum contendas mecum iudicio . . .

[13] Torréanaz, op. cit., p. 75.

(*comarcas*), were considered the highest authorities after the king. A comes is mentioned in the *fuero* of Valpuesta granted by Don Alfonso II in 804, and an armiger regis [14] also appears as member of the council. By the first third of the tenth century, we find mentioned such other officials as the mayordomus regis, the notarius regis, the comes cubiculi (master of the bedchamber, a confidential official), the escarius (steward).[15] There were sometimes several of these officials and in the reign of Don Bermudo III (1032), appears a new official, the egonomius or economus, who reappears a few years later as the royal treasurer or minister of finance, though it is not certain that he was a member of the council. In the eleventh century the council received additional members, a censor, an economus, and a *tiufado* (commander of the king's bodyguard), the *cancellario* or chancellor appears in the reign of Doña Urraca. At the same time the armiger regis disappears and the *alférez* assumes his functions.

Martínez Marina holds that the monarchs consulted the council voluntarily.[16] The kings also at various times summoned military chiefs for advice on such affairs.[17] From the time of Don Alfonso IX to Don Sancho the Brave, the assistance of the "good men" at the court was characteristic. Don Ferdinand III the Saint reorganized the officio palatino or royal council, giving it a membership of twelve and investing it with high authority, making it the highest court of appeal.[18] In 1254 the *almirante* (admiral), the *adelantado*

[14] According to Du Cange, the official who carried the shield and sword of the king.

[15] Ballesteros, II, pp. 497-8.

[16] *Ensayo Crítico sobre la legislación antigua.* In his *Teoría de las Côrtes,* he changed his mind, but here he was trying to establish an ancestry for the *Côrtes* which did not exist. His first opinion is the correct one.

[17] Torréanaz, op. cit. p. 82.

[18] Mariana holds that this council did not have jurisdiction under Don Enrique II (*Hist. gen., Lib.* xiii, c. 8), as does also Salazar de Mendoza (*Origen de las dignidades reglares de Castilla,* 1657, *Lib.* ii, c. 13, p. 56) and Padre Andrés Marcos Burriel (*Memorias para la vida del Santo Rey D. Fernando III,* 1800, *parte* I, c. xl). Torréanaz gives quotations from these authorities (pp. 117-8). Burriel gives the duties of the twelve

de la frontera (governor of a frontier province), and the *merinos mayores* [19] appear as new officials.

In 1283 the *Justicia de la casa del Rey* is named for the first time. The *Partidas* (*Segunda Partida*) name many other officials, all attending the royal council, but some assisted because of their position as palace officials and others (like the Chancellor, the notaries, secretaries, *alférez, justicia, mayordomo mayor, adelantados, merinos mayores de las comarcas, almirante*)[20] had other functions aside from their duties as members of the council. The *ricos-homes* (men of wealth), also assisted. The "good men" mentioned in various documents as attending the council, were those learned in the *fueros,* the *merinos mayores,* the *alcaldes* of the court, and others whose opinions would be considered of value. During the minorities between the reigns of Don Ferdinand IV and Don Enrique II the counsellors or deputations of *hidalgos* and good men were named by the towns and *hermandades,* though once the king was of age, he chose his own counsellors.

Don Alfonso X defined the council as follows: *Corte es llamado el lugar do es el rey, e sus vasallos con él, que le han cotianamente de consejar e de servir: . . . e otrosi ha nome an latín Curia.*[21] The *Crónica* of Don Alfonso X speaks of the monarch consulting the *infantes e ricos-homes del su consejo.* In the *Crónica* of Don Alfonso XI, describing the

men who were to act as philosophical advisers to the king in his *Nobleza y Lealtad,* which is published in his book. Don Alfonso X dismissed them and it would seem as if their work was of a temporary nature. Torréanaz also quotes Sempère, *Hist. del Derecho español* (*Lib.* II, *c.* xxi) to the effect that the organization was permanent. M. de la Fuente (*Hist. gen., parte* II, *Lib.* II, *c.* xiv) considers the twelve men of Ferdinand's creation as the beginning of the *Consejo real de Castilla.*

[19] The *merino* (word derived from the Latin term mayorino regis) was an official dating possibly from before the eleventh century. His functions were at first limited to the collection of taxes and rents. Later he was given judicial, political and military functions formerly reserved to the count and was in fact the representative of the royal authority in the *comarca.* The *merinos mayores* were later created to have jurisdiction over the *merinos* with judicial functions, Ballesteros, II, pp. 504-5.

[20] For a description of the duties of these officials, see Ballesteros, III, pp. 319-22.

[21] The *Cortes* (council, not the modern *Cortes*) is summoned to the place where the king is, and his vassals with him, where daily they have to advise him and to serve . . . and others, called in Latin, Curia (council,) *Partida Segunda Tít.* IX, *ley* xxvii.

council held in Seville before the battle of Tarifa, the king addresses the assembly in the following words: *que le aconsejasen, ca él un ome era et sin todos ellos non todia facer más que por un ome.*[22]

The daily consultation was perhaps in the nature of a private council but the full or solemn council, an assembly with the membership described above, was consulted on a wide range of interests, such as economic, administrative, political, judicial. The complexity of these interests in the later Middle Ages demanded separate councils, having nothing in common save the presidency of the king.

In the *Cortes* of Burgos (1367), Toro (1369 and 1371), Burgos (1379), petitions were presented to the king to choose good men from the cities, towns and places (*lugares*) to sit with the nobles and prelates of his council, but nothing was done until the time of Don Juan II.[23] He considered that the reform of greatest moment was to secure a great and good council in which there should be included all classes of the people, especially those on whom fell the burden and charge of the common good of the kingdom.[24] In the various *Cortes* held at Valladolid in 1385, 1387, 1407, he sought to perfect such an institution, and the reasons he gave are a matter of interest:[25] the difficulties of war, to meet the criticism that he did things on his own account without advice, because of the necessity of securing advice (as he had learned from the defeat of Aljubarrota), and lastly the principal reason, his own weakness. As finally constituted it consisted of twelve members, four prelates, four *cabelleros*, four citizens. Among the membership were to be found Pedro Tenorio, Archbishop of Toledo, renowned for his

[22] that they should advise him, because he was one man and without all of them he could not do anything more than one man, Ballesteros, III, pp. 318-9.
[23] Colmeiro, *Derecho Administrativo,* Madrid, 1876, I, p. 175.
[24] *Crónica de Don Enrique III, año 1392,* c vi.
[25] *Actas de las Córtes,* etc. II, Valladolid, 1385, p. 332.

knowledge of the law (according to Perez de Guzmán), Juan García Manrique Santiago, not less famous than Tenorio, but more of a "disturber", the Bishop of Seville and Burgos, the Marqués de Villena, and among the citizens Juan Hurtado de Mendoza—a group of most distinguished men. Their duties were to have charge of the households of the *Infantes*, to supervise the magistracies, *tenecias*, *adelantamientos*, *merinos*, *corregidores*, alms, amnesties and other favors.

The membership varied and did not always represent the estates.[26] In the minority of Don Enrique II, the *Cortes* of Valladolid and Briviesca (1391) decided that the council and not the tutors should govern the kingdom. Don Enrique III in the *Cortes* of Segovia, September 15, 1406, decided that the council should be aided by a *perlado*, two *cabelleros* and two Doctors, to prepare and draw up the petitions. The policy here instituted of bringing in lawyers or those learned in the law rather than citizens, became fixed. Men of the caliber of Pedro Sánchez de Castilla, Juan Rodríguez de Salamanca and Periañez, learned in the law, were members and were called *oidores* of the council. Don Pablo de Santa María, graduate of the University of Paris and author of the Scrutinium scriptarum, was also a member. The influence of these men, all trained in the Roman law, played a part in interpreting *Las Siete Partidas* and in molding the traditions of government along lines at variance with the earlier foundations and ideas.

During the reign of Don Juan II, the term *privada* or privy counsellor began to be used.[27] Don Alvaro de Luna, who dominated during the minority of Don Juan, took the title of *Ministro* or *Ministro mayor*.[28] He divided the council into sections, separating the administrative and

[26] Torréanaz, op. cit., p. 144.
[27] Cf. *Partida segunda, Tít.* IX, *ley* 5.
[28] Torréanaz, op. cit., p. 153, pp. 159-65.

judicial functions, which was approved by the king, thus foreshadowing the reforms of the Catholic Kings, and raised the salaries (especially his own). Though these reforms appeared plausible, they were unfavorably received, and complaints were loud that the prestige of the council had declined. It was said that it should be an honor to be counted among its membership, but the way was being opened to play favorites, particularly among the *tosca laya* (Roman lawyers), and to use the royal power as a shield for personal ambitions. Conditions were not helped by the character of Don Enrique IV, who at first heeded the petitions of his *Cortes* to restore the council as constituted in the *Cortes* of Briviesca, 1387, and Valladolid in 1442,[29] but Don Enrique was thoroughly worthless and abandoned his power and personal dignity so that the council continued to lose prestige.

To restore this was one of the major reforms of the Catholic Kings, and in the *Cortes* of Madrigal (1476), the council was definitively established.[30] It was now to consist of one prelate, two *cabelleros*, six *letrados* (lawyers), later augmented by one *cabellero* and two or three *letrados* in the *Cortes* of Toledo, when it was organized into these sections: the Council of Castile (the council of state), the Council of Finance, and the Council of Justice.[31] Aragonese affairs were handled by the Council of State. After 1480 two novelties were introduced. The head of the council was given the title of president and all members were jurists, who alone had a vote. Extraordinary counselors could be called in an occasion who might sit in while their business was being discussed but who had no vote. The Catholic Kings chose the members from the *Audiencias* and the Universities, and in

[29] *Cortes* of Toledo, 1462 in *Actas de las Cortes*, III.

[30] *Actas de las Cortes*, IV; Mariejol, *L'Espagne sous Ferdinande et Isabelle*; Colmeiro, *Derecho Administrativo*, I, p. 177.

[31] Germs for these had existed previously, see Torréanaz, pp. 196-7; Colmeiro, Introduction to *Actas de las Cortes*, p. 54.

general chose wisely.[32] The president was selected in order to have some one to preside in the absence of the king but he was only one among equals. The change from this status to one with special powers, prerogatives and salary dates from the time of the Conde-Duque de Olivares, who wheedled his way into it.[33] This precedent became habitual after the presidency of the Conde de Oropesa.

The council as now constituted had three characteristics. It was a consultive body, a tribunal of justice, and had administrative functions. The last two, of course, were the strict prerogatives of the king. He merely delegated them as a matter of convenience and the final responsibility was his. Thus we may see that although the council never lost its advisory character, the institution of the monarchy was being modified so as to permit of adaptation to the changing circumstances of an enlarged and consolidated nation. The monarch did not consider abdicating any of the functions or of dividing any of the powers traditionally associated with his office, but he was willing to reorganize his system of administration and to delegate some of his functions.

The Curia or council of the king in Aragon presents similar features to that of Castile, based on a similar tradition. The term curia was variously applied, sometimes referring to the local tribunal of administration, again meaning the council of the king, to which were summoned the magnates and prelates of the kingdom. When the chief ones of the towns were also summoned, it then took on the character of a *Cortes*, according to Longa y Bartibás. The term was also applied to the entourage of the king and to the hall in which justice was administered. The full council (plena curia) included besides the assessors and judges (the common council), the

[32] See report of Lorenzo Galindez de Cárbajal to Charles V in *Colecc. de doc. inéditos para la hist, de Españo*, vol. XX, p. 277.
[33] Cánovas del Castillo, *Historia de la Decadencia de España*. Madrid, 1910.

prelates, abbots and nobles of the kingdom who were to advise the king and approve his decisions. The members were variously named: *barones*, magnates, *próceres*, optimates, probi homines, viri regis, homines regis and boni viri. The chief official seems to have been the *mayordomo* who presided in the absence of the king.

The council was consulted on international policies, war or peace, alliances, treaties, the surrender of lands to another monarch and on giving homage to another king. Their advice was also asked on the compilation of laws or *fueros*, the abdication of the sovereign, his marriage and that of the heir, and in general on matters of administration. Appeal to the council was allowed in special instances.[34] Little change was made in the functions of the council during the latter period of the Middle Ages. Under Don Jaime I, some of its members began to form a permanent body of advisers (consilarii) attached to the palace, whose duties were fixed. Don Alfonso III reduced it to a somewhat subsidiary position for the time being, though its officials were not without considerable influence, especially the chancellor and palatine judges. The chancellor is not mentioned before the time of Don Jaime I; by the reign of Don Alfonso III he had became a highly important official, required to sign important documents, consulted on financial matters and frequently sent as ambassador. Gradually other positions in the council were created very similar to those in Castile and by 1344 the four most important were the *mayordomo*, *camalengo*, chancellor and *maestre racional* (a species of minister of finance). Cataluña and Valencia had a similar organization of their councils.[35]

[34] Ballesteros, II, pp. 622-3, summarized from Longa y Bartibás.
[35] Ballesteros, III, pp. 484-87.

THE CITY FATHERS OF BARCELONA

Chapter VII

The Municipalities

IT has been said that the *municipio* of the Middle Ages is the precursor of the modern state,[1] and the *Concejo* or municipal council is one of the most important institutions in which to study in action the development of the principles of political organization.

The ancestry of these famous councils is still the subject of research among Spanish historians, some contending that they descend from the Roman municipia as they existed anterior to the Gothic invasions in the latter days of the Empire;[2] others holding that they descend from the juridical institutions of the Hispano-Gothic state,[3] though both views ignore the decadence of the Roman municipia and the change introduced by the principles of Chrisitianity,[4] particularly during Visigothic times. The Gothic invasions wrought much destruction in the Roman organization[5] and the survival of the *Concejo* is to be sought in the *Concejo rural* which developed under the influence of the country

[1] Hinojosa, E. de, *Estudios sobre la hist. del derecho español,* p. 5.

[2] Herculano, *Historia de Portugal,* IV. Hinojosa, op. cit., pp. 9-14, disposes of the arguments of Herculano. For a fine account of the political institutions existing in Roman Spain, see Pérez-Pujol, I, pp. 127-236.

[3] Muñoz y Romero, *Discurso leido ante el Real Academia de la Historia,* 1860, pp. 38-9, 41-4.

[4] Pérez-Pujol, op. ci.t, II, p. 260, 316.

[5] Pérez-Pujol calls attention to the fact that the Roman municipal regime existed in certain places all during the Visigothic regime, and even under the Mozarabes up to the ninth century. He quotes Salviano and Idatius of the fifth century; Bishop Mintano in the sixth speaks of the municipia of Segovia, Brittablo and Cuenca; St. Ildefonso mentions them in Asturias between 530 and 560; St. Braulio and St. Isidore in the seventh century; see also Forum Iudiciorum, *Lib.* V, *Tit.* iv, *ley* 19, *Lib.* XII, *Tit.* i, *ley* 2 for traces of them (op. cit., pp. 260-61).

parishes which became the nuclei of new divisions under the traditional principles. According to Pérez-Pujol, it was at this time that the curia took on judicial and administrative functions, and the municipal corporation began to be called the *concejo general, ayuntamiento* or *consistorio.*[6]

The Arabic invasions in turn swept away much of the new organizations and when the Reconquest began to reëstablish the political institutions, the remains of the earlier institutions were not found equally preserved in all parts of the peninsula. In Septimania and Gothic Gaul where the Goths and the Hispano-Romans with their laws and judges took refuge, the Hispano-Gothic *municipio* was set up without a break. And when the people coming down from the Pyrenees established the Spanish march, the cities of Cataluña took on this form of organization.[7]

Affairs went differently in the Asturias, Galicia, León and Castile, where not a city remained in possession of the Christians, and the municipia were laid waste so that the institution was destroyed; but when the Christian power came to recover itself it took the form of the ancient tradition, and the *concejo rural* had as model the old conventus vicinorum. When a century later (824) the *fueros* and *cartas pueblas* begin to appear, the *concejo* was organized on the representative basis of the collationes or parishes, preserving the popular character which was to make eventually the Castilian *municipio* the most democratic of all those of the Middle Ages.[8]

Since there is no institution in the United States which corresponds directly to the Spanish *municipio*, and hence no word which may translate it, it is necessary to explain some-

---

[6] Ibid., p. 316.
[7] Oliver, B., *Código de las Costumbres de Tortosa*, Madrid, 1881.
[8] Pérez-Pujol, op. cit., II, p. 317-8.

what in detail what is meant by the term in Spain so that the American reader may not become confused.

The administrative unit of the Roman province in Spain was the civitas, the populus, the respublica, that is, the social group which among the peoples of the West constitute what might be called the state, under the Roman rule. This civitas embraced a nucleus of the inhabitants of the city (oppidum) and its territory, with the surrounding rural regions in which the rural population lived grouped together in towns (in Spanish *aldea*, in Latin vicus) which were sometimes fortified, or in scattered farms. In this case the inhabitants of a part of the territory of the civitas, called pagus or regio, assembled in order to transact business or to administer justice, in places called fora or conciliabula, usually located at the cross roads, called compita. This civitas is translated into Spanish *municipio*.

The rural assemblies or *concejos*—whether of the vici or pagi—were subordinate to the urban *concejos*, that is of the oppida, without losing independence in respect to economic functions, and although by the lex Julia municipalis,[9] they were under the urban *concejo* as regards the administration of justice and collection of taxes, they preserved their collective personality, independent organization and economic powers. Their general scheme was never lost during the vicissitudes of Roman reforms, and became the essential framework of the Hispano-Gothic *municipios*.[10] The classes of population to be found in the Roman municipia were the small proprietors, the coloni and the slaves, known as the plebs rustica; in the cities the rich merchants and small artisans grouped into guilds or collegia and were known as the urba plebs; and the large landed proprietors appointed

[9] Called Tabula Heracleensis, identified by Savigny with the lex Julia municipalis, cf. Pérez-Pujol, I, p. 177, note 1.
[10] Pérez-Pujol, Ibid., pp. 177-8.

to the curia, known as the ordo. It is interesting to note that with the introduction of Christianity, the curia, the plebes and the clergy elected the Bishops, and that these three classes reappear in the *concejo* of the Middle Ages.[11]

The Curia, Ordo or Senatus, was the *Concejo general* or *Ayuntamiento* of the cities of Roman Spain. Its duties were analogous to those of the Roman senate, though the magistrates were more subordinate to it than in Rome.[12] It was the chief deliberate body, having supervision over public works, games, receiving appeals from the fines imposed by the magistrates interregni, supervising finances, etc. Its powers were at their height during the second and third centuries, and under the Theodosian code it received greater powers, but under the exactions of the curiales, and during the disappearance of the middle class in the later empire the curia was thoroughly moribund by the beginning of the fifth century. Uprisings on the part of the plebs against its authority were constant before the barbarian invasions.

The most striking transformation which the municipal régime underwent during the invasions of the barbarians, may be studied in the judicial powers given to it by the *Breviario Alarico.* The ruin wrought by the invasions and the lack of culture in the new peoples, demanded a simpler organization than the old Roman legislation provided, and in the *Breviario* we find the attempt to modify it to suit the new social necessities. As many of the Roman institutions had disappeared, so were the clauses dealing with them in the Theodosian code omitted from the *Breviario.* But the municipal organization remained though much weakened.[13] Certain functions formerly assigned to the judges alone under the Roman practice, were now assigned to the judge and the

[11] Ibid, I, p. 382-3, note 4, p. 382.
[12] Mispoulet, *Les Institutions politiques des romains,* II, c. xvi, par. 94, p. 136.
[13] Pérez-Pujol, op. cit., II, pp. 285-6.

curia, so that these now formed a corporate tribunal, the *Audiencia* of that time, as Pérez-Pujol observes. The Alarican interpretation frequently translated the old judge (that is, Roman) and judgment by audientia.[14] Thus were introduced the precedents for the union of the two functions of executive (*regimiento*) and judicial, found much later in the municipal *fueros*. Savigny thinks this was introduced because it was already introduced in the Curia in later Roman days, but Pérez-Pujol considers it was the work of the Gothic invaders as a result of the necessity to fuse or at least to reconcile the institutions of the conquerors and the conquered preparatory to establishing a unified legislation, or on the strength of some other principle.[15] The curia, and the curiales, lasted until the end of the Gothic monarchy as constituted by the *Breviario Alarico* in so far as its sphere of action was concerned.[16]

The compita or rural assemblies continued to be recognized in the *Breviario* and St. Isidore describes the compita as the conventus rusticorum.[17] The Goths gave new life to this, reconstituting it for the division of land, and establish-

---

[14] Ibid., II, pp. 262, 265.

[15] According to Pérez-Pujol, when the Goths came into Spain, they already had tribunals of a judge and a certain number of auditors, chosen for each case, probably by the judge and drawn from the class of honesti or idonei. (Among the Roman Spanish, this class was the free proprietor of the Middle Ages, the class from whose ranks were recruited the curiales; among the Goths it consisted of the rich lord, master of an extensive property, the modest patron with a reduced number of clients, or even the proprietor without clients.) This precedent explains how the Gothic judges placed over the Roman Spanish instead of the former rectores imperiales, necessitated auditors with whom to consult on the law which applied to the conquered people, who were taken from the same class from which the Spanish Romans took theirs, that is, from the curiales, or honesti, idonei. In this way the curia began to intervene in the judicial power, as from the curia came those who participated with the Gothic judge in civil and criminal cases, and formed the audientia of the Romans. For discussion on this cf. Pérez-Pujol, II, pp. 266-90; and also the Forum Iudiciorum, *Lib.* VII, *Tít.* i, *ley* 5; *Lib.* VIII, *Tít.* v, *ley* 4; *Lib.* V, *Tít.* vi, *ley* 3; *Lib.* IX, *Tít.* I, *ley* 8; *Lib.* II. *Tít.* ii, *ley* 2, *Tít.* iv, *ley* 5; *Lib.* VI., *Tít.* i, *ley* 2; *Lib.* V, *Tít.* vi, *ley* 13.

[16] Pérez-Pujol, II, pp. 299-306.

[17] A law of the Theodosian code (Lib. III, Tít i, lex 2a) recognized the juridic action of this assembly by requiring that if one sold his farm, he should do it in the presence of his neighbors, to avoid fraud in the tribute. This law was incorporated in the *Breviario*. Ibid., p. 312. See also the following from St. Isidore: Compita sunt, ubi usus est conventus fieri rusticorum dicti compita, quia multa loca in agris eodem competunt, Etym. Lib. XV, c. ii, 15 (the compita are those places where it is the custom for the country people to meet together, and they are called compita because many roads in the field cross at this point and the country people assemble there).

ing it as a conventus vicinorum without disturbing its dependence upon the city as established in the Theodosian code.[18] It had charge of the division of the lands and fields, of boundaries, of pasturage, the following up of escaped slaves, of landmarks and other means of delimiting the farms, and in fact supervised all the details of rural life. This *concejo* was composed of the free men, inhabitants of the countryside, of the towns, heads of families, and it met in the streets or squares of the towns, or even at the compita or crossroads on days convenient for business.[19]

The municipal organization of the Visigothic times was incompatible with the military and semi-nomad life necessary for the Christians during the first centuries of the Reconquest. The territory under the control of the Christians in Asturias, León and Castile, formed a network of rural developments, among which appeared like islets in the sea, as Hinojosa remarked, urban centers, the residence of the court or the great ecclesiastical or lay lords, the seat of a strong fortress or a center of monastic establishment. The kingdom was divided into administrative units called comitati and comissi, which included the cities and the surrounding countryside. At the head of each was a count, who as among the Visigoths, exercised in the name of the king military, economic and judicial functions, though frequently the judicial duties were exercised by another official called a *vicario*. The count or *vicario* presided over the *Asamblea general* (or concilium) of the freemen of the territory, and heard the pleas assisted by a number of individuals called judices in the documents of the period.[20] In the ecclesiastical and lay *señorios*, the lord exercised similar functions in the

[18] See also Forum Iudiciorum, *Lib.* X, *Tit.* i, *ley* 5; *Lib.* VIII, *Tit.* v, *ley* 5; *Lib.* X, *Tit.* iii, *ley* 2. Book V discusses the topic of agriculture and throws much light on this.

[19] *F.I., Lib.* IX, *Tit* i, *ley* 8. Pérez-Pujol, II, pp. 312-15, 154-8.

[20] Hinojosa, E. de, *Estudios sobre la Hist. del derecho español,* p. 15. Pérez-Pujol, II, pp. 176-7.

Asamblea or delegated them to a villicus. These comitati and *señorios* preserved the old traditions of the Roman municipia and villa, and the *Asamblea general*, or concilium (a word used in the diplomas from the tenth century), or *concejo*, continued the traditions and functions of the conventus publicus vicinorum. It regulated trade, industry, commerce, assigned sites for the sale of various articles, fixed the price of food, supervised the products of industry, regulated the artisan guilds, and imposed fines for the violation of the municipal statutes.[21] The *concejo* also delegated two or three officials called *jurados* or *fieles* to watch over the fulfillment of the ordinances in regard to weights and measures and supplies. These held office for a year. The *concejo* could exercise original jurisdiction.

The populations of these territories were made up of diverse elements. Some existed from Roman and Visigothic times, from remains of the old Roman coloni, which term substantially reappears in the *Breviario Alarico* and the Forum Iudiciorum, although the latter does not use the term colonus once.[22] Other settlements arose spontaneously as it were around some site favored for trade, or in the shadow of some monastery. These were encouraged either because they were on strategic sites, or suitable for securing large loans and taxes so necessary for the carrying on of the Wars of the Reconquest. Many Mozarabes [23] joined them, fleeing from the Moorish domination into the Christian lands. Such were the elements of the population in many places settled throughout Galicia, the central part of old Castile as Burgos,

[21] Hinojosa, Ibid., p. 20, quoting *fueros* of Leon (1020), Nájera (1001-35), and others. See note 1.

[22] Pérez-Pujol, op. cit., IV., pp. 232-9. In a document dating from 745 describing the refounding of Lugo, the inhabitants who founded and endowed the church are called famuli ex familia Odoarii episcopi, but they are true coloni, according to Pérez-Pujol, for they paid a fixed rent for the land they cultivated, like the ancient coloni, had property, since they gave to the church the fifth part of their personal property and of their lands. See also Isidore, Etymol., Lib. IX, c. iv, num. 36 and following.

[23] Mozarabes were Christians living among the Moors.

the mountains of Sántander and part of the Basque lands during the reigns from Don Alfonso the Catholic to Don Ordoño II. The social classes were very much the same as those found in the Roman and Gothic days: freemen, members of the curiales, judges (alone eligible for public services and subject to the tribute), coloni, freed men and slaves.[24]

The necessity of reconciling such diverse elements and securing justice for each, demanded rules of administration for the conduct of business, construction of public works and above all administration in the realm of justice, beyond the power of the *concejo* as then constituted to accomplish. In the *señorios* there were frequent abuses of power on the part of the lords, lay and ecclesiastical, who had full jurisdiction, civil and criminal, in virtue of their character as representing the king.[25]

---

[24] Pérez-Pujol, IV, pp. 91-290.

[25] The *señorios* appear first in Asturias. A charter of 804, granted by Don Alfonso II to the Church of Valpuesta, though this is not the first example, is a grant of the sovereign for the salvation of his soul. They were also granted as a reward for services. They were conceded either to lay or ecclesiastical lords, more often to the latter, for the greater security arising from the permanency of these, and conferred on the lord the right to

1 receive the tribute or services owed by the inhabitants to the sovereign
2 administer justice within the territory
3 collect the fines due the monarch
4 receive the bonds or securities as guarantees for judicial composition
5 administrative power
6 require military services from the inhabitants
7 name functionaries who would take the place of those of the king.

The lord by this was not emancipated from the jurisdiction of the king. He had the status of what might be called the governor of the district, and the king continued to exercise supreme power (Cardenas, *Ensayo sobre la historia de la propriedad territoral en España*, I, pp. 342-3.

Such grants were given frequently during the first four centuries of the Reconquest, but did not have the character which Feudalism assumed in other countries, although French influence is seen in the eleventh century, with the marriage of the King with Doña Constanza and of their daughters to Burgundian nobles. The French feudal ideas also crept in with the monks of the Cluniac reform and French priests who came in with Don Bernado, Archbishop of Toledo. The franchises began to read, the granting of the land "with all its dominion and *señorios* with whatever pertains to the royal voice, with all *fuero* and right, according to the correspondence of the royal power." The concession then had the effect of creating around the royal sovereignty, little sovereignties, varying with the importance of the grantees, the ecclesiastical receiving the greater degree of independence.

The lord had to give homage to the king even when he had legislative power. This was exercised in conjunction with the *concejo*, the abbot with the council of his convent, the Bishop with the *cabildo*. The legislation was in the name of the king.

The lord was a judge in the first instance, and also of appeal, and the royal justice intervened only when the justice of the lord failed. Some lords had final appeal. No documents deprived the king of all his prerogatives, and the lord was obliged to accept the royal coinage (save the prelate of Compostella, 1108, Abbots of Sahagún, 1116, the

The twelfth century saw a great increase in the development of industry and commerce, and brought new life and strength to these territories, demanding changes in the organization. As centers of industrial activity, the towns acquired an economic importance which called for a wider frame for their political organization. The king saw in their increasing wealth and development a new aid with which to secure funds for their long wars against the Moors and a check on the rising spirit of independence among the nobles. With these changes in the significance of these urban centers or *municipios*, to give them their ancient name, came the opportunity for the *concejo* to assume wider powers, and the development of the municipalities was no other than the attempt of the *concejos* to take on administrative and judicial functions.[26]

The *fuero* of Villavicencio of the eleventh century reveals the *concejo* as a corporative entity with powers to proceed against the judges who might abuse their powers, and adjudges also to the *concejo* a part of the fines collected in various cases, for example, for not attending the *concejo* when summoned or the *Asamblea general.* The *fuero* of Sépulveda of 1076 grants to the *Concejo* the right of inheriting the property of those dying without heirs (si non habuerunt gentes, hereditent eum conceio, et faciunt inde elemosina pro sua anima).[27]

The *fuero* of León in 1020 recognizes the autonomy of the *concejo* in assuring it its own judges. The *municipio* now appears as a distinct entity in the territory of the count but

Church of San Antolin de Palencia), to serve the king with arms, to respect his treaties and international obligations, attend the curia or *cortes*, and he was never considered on an equality with the king, who could exile him if he wished (summarized from *La Potestad real y los Señorios,* by Claudio Sánchez-Albornoz in *Revista de Archivos, bibliotecas y museos,* Sept.-Dec., 1914.)

[26] Hinojosa, op. cit., pp. 25-6.

[27] Muños y Romero, *Col. de Fueros,* I, pp. 174, 285. If they have no family, the council shall inherit it, and from it shall take alms for his soul.

not under his jurisdiction, and the *fueros* applied equally to all the inhabitants as may be seen from the *fuero* of Palenzuela (1074): Unusquis vestrum sive infançon sive villano qui voltam habuerit intus villam, habeat aut unum forum; extra villam, habeant sua omnia,[28] and that of Sahagún (1115): Et quicumque nobilis vel cuiuslibet dignitas in villa Sancti Facundi in propria vel in aliena dono habitaverit; ipse et quicumque cum eo fuerit habeat forum ville sicut unusquisque de vicinis,[29] and in the *fuero* of Miranda (1099): Et omnes populatores qui modo sunt aut de cetero homines generosi aut pedoni aut mauri aut iudei habeant istum forum[30] and in that of Villadiego (1134): Similiter illos cavelleros et illos infançones per livores et per todos directos, de pretio habeant unum forum cum illos villanos.[31]

It is to be noted that in the last two statements, the great principle of the Forum Iudiciorum, the supremacy of law, is clearly stated to apply to all the people, including Moors and Jews and to all classes of the people.[32] There are also the guarantee of rights for the citizens of the *municipios*: no one could be punished without due process (*sin forma de pro-*

---

[28] Muños y Romero, Ibid., p. 276. All of you whether *infante* or inhabitant of the *municipio* who dwell within the *municipio* shall have the one *fuero*, without the *municipio* each shall have his own.

[29] Muños y Romero, Ibid., p. 309. And whichever noble or whatever dignity in the *municipio* of Sahagún, whether he lives in his own house or with another, he and whoever shall be with him, shall have the *fuero* of the municipio, and also each one from the neighbors around.

[30] Ibid., p 351. And all the inhabitants, of one kind or another, whether homines generosi, or pedoni, Moors or Jews, shall have this *fuero*.

[31] Hinojosa, *Estudios Críticos sobre el derecho español.*

[32] The *fuero* of Toledo is particularly worthy of note. Reduced to Christian rule by Don Alfonso VI in 1085, it was the most precious gain of the Reconquest up to that date. By the terms of the capitulation, the Arab population was granted the practice of its religion and its laws. The same privilege was extended to the Jews. The Christian elements were represented by the Castilian and the Mozarabes, All Christians were admitted to vote. The government of the city was entrusted to two *alcaldes*, one Mozarabe and one Castilian, elected by the majority of each class. The Mozarabes used the Forum Iudiciorum and had more extensive jurisdiction in cases between Christians and Jews or Moors. The Castilian *alcalde* used the *Fuero Viejo de Castilla.* The municipal corporation took the name *ayuntamiento*, and not *concejo*, since the Arab population was so superior to the Christian that the Moors were *concejo*, according to the expression used in the *Crónica de López de Ayala.* The *fuero* of Toledo was extended to Escalona, Talavera and the cities of Andalusia. The Arabs and Jews sought shelter here under the protection of the Kings of Castile (Sebastián y Martínez, A., *Municipalidades de Castilla y León*, Madrid, 1877, pp. 127-8.

ceso), a right which though often violated was upheld by the representatives of the cities in the *Cortes* and there recognized by the kings. Nor could one be imprisoned without an order from the judge, and not then without sufficient guarantees. One could not build within the limits of the jurisdiction of the *concejo* without its consent, nor could a citizen sell his lands to inhabitants of other cities or to powerful lords.[33] The inviolability of domicile and property was recognized, the municipal administration was guaranteed by right application of the laws, the *merinos* and *sayones* (judges) of the king were forbidden to enter any house in León without permission of the magistrate, the rights of married women were guarded against the abuses of their husbands.[34]

The power to grant *fueros* was tacitly considered implied in the grant of privileges conceded by the king to the holders of the *señorios* inasmuch as by this they participated in the power of the king, and so the lords, lay and ecclesiastical, abbots and masters of the military orders were accustomed to grant *fueros* within the limits of their jurisdictions.[35]

While the increase in the *fueros* and the development of the municipal régime worked a gradual and steady improvement in the social and political conditions, raising the status of the rural classes [36] and providing the citizens with clearer definitions of their rights and ever broader ideas of independence, the development did not proceed equally throughout all the *municipios*. For it must be kept in mind that the liberty recognized by the Spaniard of the Middle Ages was still the liberty of the traditional Forum Iudiciorum and of the philosophy of Augustine. It was not a liberty for the individual as an individual, in the modern sense, it was still

[33] Martínez-Marina, *Ensayo Hist. Crítico sobre la antigua legislación*, pp. 122-54; also Hinojoso, op. cit., p. 28.
[34] Sebastián y Martínez, Ibid., pp. 96 sq.
[35] Hinojosa, op. cit., p. 29.
[36] Hinojosa, Ibid., pp. 37-43.

the liberty of the individual as an individual in his relationships with other individuals and in their mutual relations to God; and the individual was guaranteed his rights to the point where he had the necessary freedom to carry out the obligations arising out of this network of relationships.

As Hinojosa remarks,[37] "The liberty which the men of the Middle Ages enjoyed was not a quality recognized in all as inherent in his condition as a man or a citizen; it was a series, a gradation of particular liberties conceded by special title to the class of which he formed a part. The striking characteristic of the municipal organization is then particularity and diversity. Each city acquires separately its privileges, receives its peculiar constitution and has its own physiognomy. The franchise granted to the various towns differ in quantity and in extension."

True, because what was conceded to one was not necessarily conceded to all since what was granted to one was granted because of the special needs arising out of the special circumstances created by the special relationships of that particular place. If similar relationships requiring similar regulations to secure the justice which a due harmony of these relationships demanded, existed in other places, then similar "privileges" as Hinojosa calls them could be granted. And as the relationships extended into other areas and the creation of new communities of interests developed into new relationships, the people's conception of how much freedom of action was necessary in order to control these relationships, widened, and we have the period which is called in history the struggle for civil and political emancipation.

Conflicts of jurisdiction arose between the economic and political spheres, and later between the political and ecclesi-

[37] Hinojosa, Ibid., p. 42.

astical in order to define more exactly their respective jurisdictions. Conflicts which at first were over points of jurisdiction, insensibly changed into conflicts in respect to principle as the alien Roman law was gradually appealed to in the interpretation of the difficulties. The original institutions not being based upon the old Roman law directly, as a result of this reversal could only fall into ruin or stiffen into ineptitude. It was not so much that the original institution was inadequate for the strain time puts on everything, but that adapted by the very principles of its being to a particular end it could no longer pursue that end when its underlying principles were changed.

The first step in this long drama is taken in the struggle created in the ecclesiastical *señorios* by the desire of the inhabitants of the *municipios* to abolish the distinction between their inhabitants and those of the ecclesiastical *señorios.* As the economic interests began to embrace and include the two entities, the distinctions had become a source of disturbance. The corporative property of the Church, and also the private property of the ecclesiastics, were exempt from the municipal taxes. The rural and domestic servitors of the ecclesiastics, frequently enjoyed the personal exemptions of their masters,[38] and the *municipios* wished to abolish this distinction and bring all under the unity of the *fuero.* The *concejo* wished to assume certain powers exercised by the ecclesiastical lords. In the towns and cities of such ecclesiastical *señorios* as Sahagún, Santiago, Lugo, Orense, Tuy, Palencia, Zamora, for examples, the citizens wished to transfer from the lord to the *concejo* the nomination of the municipal magistrates and to narrow the sphere of ecclesiastical jurisdiction in civil matters.

The bitterness with which the struggle was carried on

[38] Hinojosa, Ibid., p. 46.

in the town of Sahagún from 1087 to 1322 illustrates the force economic interests had at that time. The struggle opened with the attempt of the burgesses to abolish the *mañería* (this permitted the lord to inherit the property of one dying without children), to abolish the privileges the monks had of first choice in the buying of articles under pain of fine and confiscation, and to abolish the seignorial monopolies of the oven and sale of wine, and to remove the town from the jurisdiction of the monastery. Don Alfonso VI suppressed the uprising, and abolished in 1096 and 1110 the oven monoply and the *mañería.* Further uprising took place under Don Alfonso the *Batallador*, Don Alfonso VII, St. Ferdinand III and Don Alfonso the Wise. The *fuero* was then modified to permit the burgesses to appeal to the king from the decisions of the abbot, and allowed greater facilities for the sale of lands. In 1322 Don Alfonso XI decided that the *alcaldes* should be elected from a list drawn up by the Abbot from a list previously drawn up by the *concejo.*

The struggle in Santiago was carried on between the Archbishop and the *cabildo* on the one hand and the *concejo* on the other all during the reigns of Don Ferdinand the Saint to that of Don Juan II in order to free the town from the jurisdiction of the Archbishop, never entirely succeeding. Sometimes the struggle took on a personal character as when the clergy and the people united against the attempts of the famous Gelmirez in 1116 and 1136 to become the governor of the city.[39] Success fluctuated, now on one side now on the other, and the kings frequently took sides to favor their own interests, so that the story is confused and it is difficult to tell how much was gained and how much was lost in either case. Custom had a strong hold upon the people

[39] For an account of similar struggles in Lugo, Tuy, Orense, and others, cf. Hinojosa, Ibid., pp. 52-65.

and it would appear that neither side was anxious for a complete victory. The struggles almost always turned upon a particular point, collection of a tax, or exercise of authority. It was not until that unhappy thing, specialization of function, differentiation of the organism, began to creep in, either as a result of the passion to organize details, or of the increasing complexity of the relationships created by the greater wealth and security of the towns, that the simple forms of the earlier *municipios* of the tenth to the twelfth centuries began to break up.[40]

During the thirteenth century new *municipios* were formed for the important cities of Córdova, Seville, Murcia, Carmona, Jérez and Cádiz. The *fueros* of the first two were granted by Don Ferdinand III and for the others by Don Alfonso X. In order to facilitate the repopulation, new towns were also established with *fueros* such as Villa Real (Ciudad Real).

The constitutions of the *municipios* reveal essentially democratic features. All the inhabitants were eligible for the municipal offices. In the ecclesiastical *señorios*, though the citizens did not elect the officials, they frequently presented lists of those eligible. The names, attributes and number of the municipal offices varied with the towns. Sometimes, as in Santiago, Tuy or Oviedo, they were called *justicias*, in others *alcaldes*. In the *fuero* of Murcia, the inhabitants were permitted to name annually two judges, a *justicia* and a *fiel almotacén*, to govern the city. These were elected by the *cabelleros* and "good men." These last could name six *jurados* who under the direction of the *alcaldes* and *alguaciles* constituted the *ayuntamiento*.[41] Don Sancho IV in the *Cortes*

---

[40] Among the *señorios* there was a special kind called *Behetrías*, peculiar to Castile. These were midway between a *concejo* and a dependent *señorio*. They were grouped around a chief in the old German style, elected their lords, and were called *benefactoria* or *abolenga* also, because of the power to elect the lords from a certain family.

[41] Ballesteros, III, p. 342.

of Palencia (1286) promised to the *municipios* to remove the *alcaldes* and *justicias*, appointed by the king and called *mayorales* and *guardianes*, though he reserved the right to name such if petitioned to do so by the towns.[42] Ballesteros considers this as a breach in the democratic system and a wedge for the king later on to appoint the *alcaldes* or *jueces de salario*, the *alcaldes veedores* and then the *corregidores.* But this interpretation, giving the idea of the encroachment of royal power, does not take into consideration the traditional view of the king in his function of giving justice. The king could never abdicate his duty in this respect, nor could his people expect him to, and hence it would happen that the people would desire the royal judges. The *merino* or *mayordomo* was the royal judge. The *sayón* was a local judge, an official which had continued from Visigothic days. In the towns and cities directly dependent upon the king, there were special officials to collect the crown rents.

Don Alfonso X regulated the organization of the *ayuntamientos* of León and Castile. In the *fuero* of Seville, the *alcaldes, escribanos* and *jurados* were royal appointees. The constitution of the *ayuntamiento* of Burgos provided that sixteen *vecinos,* with the *alcaldes ordinarios* and *merino mayor,* should administer the affairs of the *municipio* and "those things which they should understand as in our service, and for the protection of the said city" (*aquellas cosas que entendieren que es más nuestro servicio é por é guarda de la dicha ciudad*). This is a further manifestation of the traditional view that the king was charged with justice and administration of the affairs of his people. Don Alfonso XI instituted for Segovia *regidores,* later extended to other towns, with right of popular election.[43]

---

[42] Ballesteros, III, p. 342.
[43] Ballesteros, III, pp. 343-4, for further account of municipal officials.

In the twelfth and thirteenth centuries, the *Asamblea general* of the *municipio* on a mandate from the *concejo* exercised police administration, judicial and military functions. During this period also began the division of society into classes of *cabelleros* and *peones*,[44] though the former had no monopoly of the offices, nor were the inhabitants of the towns and rural districts at a disadvantage with those of the cities or chief city of the *municipio*.[45]

At the beginning of the fourteenth century the *concejo* began to supplant the *Asamblea general*, though this continued to flourish even into the nineteenth century.[46] The *concejo* or municipal council [47] was to be consulted if any change was to be made in the status of the *municipio*.[48] All of the inhabitants, broadly speaking, were represented in the council.[49] They assembled in open council (*concejo abierto*). This assembly discussed and decided local affairs, inspected the administration and elected the magistrates by majority vote. It was summoned and presided over by the judges or foral *alcaldes*. The difficulties of the *concejo abierto* forced the *concejo cerrado*, to whom were admitted only the magistrates. The municipal corporation consisting of the judges, foral *alcaldes*, *jurados*,[50] was charged with the government as described in the *fuero*. It formed a delibera-

---

[44] For an interesting account of the crystallization of the social classes as they appear in the *Poema del Cid*, see Hinojosa, *Estudios sobre la hist. del derecho español*, pp. 73-78. See also Ballesteros, II, pp. 519-23; III, pp. 348-59.

[45] *Fuero* of León, 1020.

[46] Hinojosa, Ibid., p. 68, note 1.

[47] Sometimes the Spanish use the term *concejo* as synonym for *municipio*, Spanish for municipium, and sometimes for the council, that is for the *Asamblea general* of the *municipio*.

[48] *Cortes* of Valladolid, 1293, 1295, 1297. *En el libro fuero ninguno cosa non raa nin escriba sin mandamiento del rei y de todo el conceio.*

[49] For the constitution of the municipal corporations see Sebastián y Martínez, *Municipalidades de Castilla y León*, pp. 184-94.

[50] The *jurados* were those charged with the defense of the municipal corporation and of the citizens against all illegal extension of the authority of the magistrates. All cities and towns of the *realengo* had them. They were elected like the *alcaldes*, usually two in number. When acting together, they were termed the *cabildo de jurados*. They met weekly and *alcaldes* were forbidden to assist at the meetings. They could assist at the meetings of the *concejo*, and represent the *municipio* in the *cortes*. One *procurado* had to be a *jurado*. It was considered a great honor to be chosen a *jurado*.

tive assembly and a tribunal for justice. There was no set time for meeting, but it could meet on call when necessary. The deliberations were public, though secret sessions were held. The *sayón* was responsible for order. As a juridic person the *municipio* had rights and duties, could hold property, though the king could grant its land to private persons. This was dangerous to the independence of the *municipio* since it weakened it, and it was forbidden in the *Cortes* of 1295, conceded again in the *Cortes* of *Alcalá*, 1348, but withdrawn in the *Cortes* of Toro, 1371 and Valladolid in 1442.

Early in the fourteenth century also, the municipal offices came to be the exclusive privilege of the *cabelleros* or privileged class. In the *Ordenamiento* of Don Ferdinand III in 1250 for the town of Uceda, it was forbidden to admit the tradespeople in the *concejo* as this would detract from its dignity, and only *cabelleros* or substantial citizens were to be admitted. In 1332 Don Alfonso XI forbade the tradespeople to form part of the *ayuntamiento* as the *concejo* then began to be called, or to hold office.[51] The net result of this was to place the inhabitants of the towns and the countryside on a basis of inequality in relation to the rights and duties before the inhabitants of the capital city and to exclude them from all efficacious share in the government. Here was introduced a wedge that was to upset that delicate balance of interests on which the whole frame of the medieval government rested. In the economic order now instead of being exploited by the lords, their class was to be exploited by the *concejo.*

To the struggle to regulate the due relationships of the *municipio*, succeeded the struggle for power among the cities of Castile, which struggle often caused more bloodshed and bitterness than the earlier ones to delimit the jurisdictions.

[51] Hinojosa, Ibid., p. 68, note 2.

This situation arose in part from the creations of the *Hermandades.* During the reign of Don Alfonso X, a tendency arose for various of the *municipios* to form a union. In the *Cortes* of 1252, 1258, 1268, he prohibited these (*las confradías et juras malas*) as illegal. In 1282 during the uprisings in favor of the pretensions of Don Sancho, the prelates, rich men, *cabelleros* and *concejos* formed the powerful *Hermandad de Castilla, León y Galicia.* The idea of the *Hermandades* had its origin in the *fuero* of Salamanca in which the common interest of Arévalo, Medina del Campo, Olmedo, Coca, Toro Zamora, Segovia, Sepúlveda, Toledo, Palencia, León and Burgos were recognized. A *hermandad* of the bee-keepers and bow-men of Talavera, Toledo and Villareal against the incursions of bandits was approved by both Don Ferdinand III and Don Alfonso X. Similar *hermandades* were formed in 1295 against the demands of the nobles. They were common during the minority of Don Alfonso XI to check the usurpations of the nobles. Don Enrique II recognized them in the *Cortes* of Toro, 1370, and Don Juan I permitted them representation in the *Cortes* of Segovia in 1386, though this privilege was withdrawn in the *Cortes* of Guadalajara in 1390. In general it may be said that the kings favored them whenever they were of assistance in maintaining order, and opposed them when they became the prey of rival factions and the manifestations of jealousy among the cities. The *Cortes* of Toledo in 1462 complained to Don Enrique IV of the exactions of these, and in order to legitimize and regulate them, the *Santa Hermandad* of the Kingdom of Castile and León was recognized in 1465, the principal mission of which was to maintain order.

The centralizing tendencies of the Roman law caused the officials to seek to take from the *concejo* its judicial functions and to intervene directly in the life of the *municipio*. Powerful families and individuals began to exploit the *municipios* for their own personal aggrandizement. Once the distinction between *cabelleros* and *peones* was recognized, the former began to look for a position in the *concejo* as their right. In Soria three *cabelleros* were always members of the *concejo*, selected from the twelve major families of the city. In León one of the *alcaldes* was to be a *cabellero*, in Toledo three *fieles* were selected from the same class. In Arévalo the five families who supported Don Enrique de Trastamara selected the officials of justice. This custom spread and gradually a class of *cabellería villana* grew up, and in the pursuit of the municipal offices, gave origin to bloody contests among rival families. The Ayalas and Silvas fought in Toledo, the Tovares and Reoyos in Valladolid, the Nieblas and Marchenas, the Arcos and Medina Sidonias in Seville, to mention but a few. These struggles were frequently carried from the town into the *municipios* at large, and wars were started among them, such as between Oviedo and Avilés, and between Zamora and Salamanca in the fourteenth century. By the fifteenth these municipal contentions had produced a state of affairs bordering on anarchy and this with the consequent confusion in the municipal finances brought in the intervention of the king.[52]

The towns and cities which had endeavored to escape the exactions of the seignorial régime by placing themselves under the protection of the sovereign found themselves during the reigns of such kings as Don Enrique IV and Don Juan II, handed over to favorites on whom were conferred the rights of jurisdiction. And the interference of the royal power in the elections of representatives to the *cortes*, so corrupted the government of the *municipios* that these easily

[52] Ballesteros, III, p. 344.

deserved the contempt with which they were regarded by those imbued with absolutist ideas of the king's sovereignty so popular during the sixteenth and seventeenth centuries. The parliamentary régime so foreign to their original idea which was introduced later, completed their ruin. The point of departure for this sad fate came at the moment that the Roman law idea of sovereignty as a matter of will of the administrator, began to displace the old Spanish idea of sovereignty as the authority or final arbiter in regulating the relations of individuals or social classes in view of the final aims of justice.

Though the decline of the municipal institution did not result immediately from the introduction of the Roman law theory, the steps in its decline led directly to a situation in which the Roman theory might seem to find justification, and therefore real reform of the *municipio* on the old Spanish theory became impossible. Once the control of the government of the *municipio* passed from the *concejo abierto* to the *ayuntamiento,* the path was open to the rival ambitions of the nobles. The exactions of the *ayuntamientos* then became personal and the people began to be exploited. The tradition of the *municipio* as a territorial unit and a place in which were resolved the various interests of the inhabitants was confused. So that as a result, the *municipio* so democratic in the Middle Ages, because it was a product of the Christianized-social forces of the times, returned to the bureaucratic model of pagan Rome and perished.

Not as many studies of the *municipios* of the eastern kingdoms have been made as for the western, but the origins of the *municipios* of Aragon and Navarre, generally considered, are similar to those of Castile and León. The sources of study are the *fueros* of Daroca (1114), Calatayud (1131) and Teruel (1176), the last being the most complete of the *fueros* of Aragon. In the common type of *municipio* (such as that of Saragossa), we find as in Castile, the parish as a kind of electoral college, with all the inhabitants voters and eligible for office. The *asamblea general* called *concello* was presided over by the *jurados*, elected by the parish. The *jurado* had functions similar to those of the Castilian *jurado*. Local affairs were handled by the *cabildo municipal*, formed by the *jurados*. The list of municipal officials corresponds closely in function to those of Castile, though Añade Ribera rather holds to the influence of Moorish institutions.

According to Galo Sánchez, the *municipios* of Aragon may be divided into classes, some purely Aragonese in origin, some showing the Catalan rather than the Castilian influence, and others the Castilian rather than the Catalan. The *fuero* of Teruel on which the *fuero* of Cuenca was modeled, has all the democratic features of the Castilian institution. Navarre, so long associated with Aragon, reflects its customs. The *comunidades* were characteristic of Aragon. The city (*ciudad*) with its surrounding settlements (*aldeas*) formed the *comunidad*, on the plan somewhat of the Castilian *municipio*. It was directly under the king, and not a feudal *señorio*, was divided into six cantons called *sexma*, and was a cross between the modern province and the ancient *alfoz*. At its head was a magistrate (*procurado general*), elected by the *jurados* of the towns forming the *comunidad*. During the twelfth century the Aragonese *municipio* reached its height, the *comunidad* showing most complete democratic features. Saragossa represented the aristocratic model and Jaca was more dependent upon the king. The further progress of these *comunidades* was checked by the influence of feudalism.[53]

A similar development in Aragon may be noted to that in Castile. In the thirteenth century, Don Jaime I entrusted

[53] Ballesteros, II, pp. 625-8.

the government of the city to the city itself. Thus the municipal corporation, assuming the authority of the *municipio*, communicated directly with the king and the royal officials could not exercise jurisdiction within the *municipio*. The settlements were divided into *ciudades, villas, lugares*, the first only having representation in the *cortes*. Such were Calatayud, Daroca, Teruel and Borja. The political unit of the *municipio* remained the parish. Whoever resided for a year within the boundaries of the *municipio* was a citizen. The citizen in general enjoyed the suffrage, active and passive, though some places had various restrictions and property qualifications. The *concejo* or *plega* was the assembly of all the citizens. Owing to disturbances frequently arising in this, its functions gradually fell to the *cabildo municipal* or *concejo;* which was the assembly of the most important citizens of each parish. Rarely in Aragon did the *municipios* quarrel with each other.

In Cataluña the municipal organization was uniform, with a grand council, formed of the greatest possible number of representatives of the neighborhood. The smallest settlements sent heads of families as representatives; in the cities the number was limited by royal decree. In Barcelona there were a hundred. Unions of *municipios* in Cataluña were very ancient and frequent. They were of various kinds and received various names, such as *corregatges, federacions de pobles, lligues, patzeríes.*[54]

---

[54] Ballesteros, III, pp. 500-3.

SPANISH LAWGIVERS

Chapter VIII

The *Cortes*

THE *cortes* as an institution of government in which were represented all classes of the people, namely the clergy, the nobles, the *municipios,* cannot be said to have existed until the *Cortes* of León in 1188. In this the word curia was used instead of concilium.[1] The Latin text reads: in plena curia, translated into Spanish *en cumplida corte.* The *Cortes* of Benevente (1202) and of León (1208) are also clearly the meeting of the three estates. The first *Cortes* of Castile to have this character was the *Cortes* of Seville in 1250, wherein also the masters of the military orders participated for the first time,[2] and from then on both León and Castile had representatives from the three estates.

Don Alfonso II the Chaste fixed his court at Oviedo [3] but none of the councils summoned by him or his successors had the character of a *cortes.* Don Alfonso V summoned the bishops, abbots and nobles to discuss the spiritual and temporal affairs of the kingdom, and restored the Gothic laws, according to Archbishop Rodrigo.[4] The term *cortes* and *ayuntamiento* was applied by Ambrosio de Morales to the assembly of bishops, abbots, counts and gentlemen in which

[1] Curia may mean a palace or a court, that is, where the king has his residence, Colmeiro, *Cortes de los antiguos reinos de León y Castilla,* Madrid, 1883-4, I, pp. 11, 12. Curia was applied to the *cortes* in imitation of the thirty curiae into which the Roman people were divided, Caroleu e Inglada, Pella y Forgas, *Las Córtes Catalanas,* Barcelona, 1876.

[2] Colmeiro, *Cortes de los antiguos reinos de León y Castilla,* I, p. 13.

[3] Omnem Gothorum ordinem, sicuti Toledo fuerat tam in Ecclesia, quam Palatio in Oveto cuncta, Colmeiro, Ibid., I, p. 4.

[4] Ibid., p. 7.

Don Ferdinand I the Great was crowned and annointed, but this was not a true *cortes*. The transition from the council to the *cortes* took place undoubtedly between 1020 and 1188, though the details are obscure.[5] In the councils of Oviedo, 1115, the oath introduced to observe all the statutes, was subscribed to by all the subjects of the Queen, Doña Urraca, which recognizes the people as part of the nation with the clergy and nobility. During the reign of Don Alfonso VI, though his assemblies were mixed, separate ecclesiastical synods were frequently called, sometimes by the Pope, sometimes presided over by the Legate. The Spanish Church was enthusiastic for the views of Pope Gregory VII, hence the summoning of these synods.[6] The kings continued to call the mixed councils necessary under feudal conditions. As clergy and nobles crystallized into estates, and therefore representative of social interests, the councils had to reflect the changes. The *Cortes* of Nájera in 1137 or 1138 was an example. This was called a *cortes* in the *Ordenamiento de Alcalá* and in the *Fuero Viejo de Castilla.* The *Cortes* of Benevente (1202) and of León (1208) also had representatives of the three estates.

Various views are current among the historians as to the cause of the change from the mixed councils to the *cortes.* Colmeiro holds that this was due to the influence of Pope Gregory VII, anxious to withdraw the Church from any suspicion of temporal control, and to the attitude of the famous Bishop Diego Gelmírez. The Councils of Burgos (1136), of Valladolid (1137), Palencia (1148) were purely ecclesiastical, though on account of the civil interests of the clergy in the *señorios,* they continued to sit in the *cortes* as representative of such interests. *Municipios* were formed

[5] Pérez-Pujol, op. cit., III, p. 337, note 4. For discussion on the question whether the Councils of Toledo were true *cortes* or not, pp. 326-33.

[6] Colmeiro, op. cit., I, p. 10.

in León earlier than in Castile, and so the *cortes* as representative of the three estates appeared there first.

The nobility was represented by the so-called *ricos omes*, and among them the *Infantes* had the first place. The representation of the popular class differed slightly in that its powers were delegated, though the nobility as well as the clergy could be represented indirectly by a *procurador* as in the case of the *municipios*. The clergy was represented by the archbishops, bishops and masters of the military orders. The representatives of the popular class were usually called *procuradores*, sometimes *mandatarios* or *mensajeros*. In some *cortes* they received the generic name of *omes-bonos*. The sovereigns did not grant representation to all the *concejos*, and thus the representation varied. In the *Cortes* of Burgos, (1315) for example, over 100 *procuradores* from the cities and towns attended. As representation was a privilege, the towns which had it did not wish it extended, and others were unwilling to assume with it the burdens of the expense. The *procuradores* were chosen either by election, by lot, or by the *turno* (alternately) from among the most responsible men of the *municipios*. They were remunerated and their expenses paid.[7]

Few important studies have been made on the origins of the Aragonese *cortes*. Don Vicente La Fuente considers the Council of Jaca in 1060 as the first authentic *cortes*, though the Academy of History recognizes that of Don Ramírez in 1071 as the first. At Jaca the king, Don Ramírez I, assisted and his son Don Sánchez Ramírez, and important bishops and magnates. Notable also is the presence of the people, men and women, approving the acts of the council.[8] La Fuente also recognizes as a true *cortes*, the Council of Jaca in 1064,

[7] Ballesteros, III, p. 330-33.

[8] Audientes enim cuncti habitores Aragonum regni tam viri quam feminae, omnes una voce laudantes Deum confirmaverunt dicentes. Ballesteros, II, p. 624.

though the Academy of History does not. Zurita says that in the *Cortes* of Huesca in 1162 the *procuradores* of the cities and towns of the kingdom had representatives for the first time. Frelín says this *cortes* also included representatives from Navarre. The development of the *cortes* in Aragon followed the same stages as in Castile, that is from the mixed assemblies to those purely civil. Here too as in Castile, the *cortes* was considered the "synthetic representation of the organic diversity of the social factors of the kingdom," in the words of Manuel Bofarull y Sarret.[9]

In the Aragonese *Cortes* there were four estates: the upper nobility, the *ricos hombres*, descendants of early conquerors; the lower nobility, divided into *mesnaderos*, originating in the household of Don Jaime the Conqueror, the *cabelleros*, the household titles, the *infanzones* or sons of knights; the clergy; the burgesses or *universidades*, representatives of the towns and cities. The *procuradores* of the *universidades* were elected by all the *vecinos* of the towns and cities. As a rule they enjoyed full liberty, though at times they went with secret or reserved instructions.[10]

In the middle of the twelfth century Aragon incorporated into her realms all the territories of Cataluña. These however preserved their own laws and customs, the union being personal, that is confined to the person of the king. The first true *cortes* in Cataluña was held in 1283 under Don Pedro the Great when the rule was laid down to summon it annually,[11] though from the time of Don Ramón Berenguer,

[9] Ballesteros, III, p. 495.

[10] Ibid.

[11] *Una vez el año en aquel tiempo que nos parecerá mas oportuno, nos y succesores celebrarémos dentro de Cataluña Corte general á las Catalanes en la cual con nuestro prelados religiosas, barones, cabelleros, ciudadanos y hombres de villas tratemos del buen estado y reformación de la tierra; cuya Corte non seamos tenidos á hacer ni celebrar si nos lo impidiese una justa razón*, Las Cortes Catalanas, p. 19 (Once a year at that time which will appear to us most opportune, we and our successors shall celebrate within Cataluña a general *cortes* for the Catalans, in which, with our prelates, barons, knights, citizens and men of the towns, we shall treat of the general welfare and of reforms for the land, and only a just reason shall prevent the holding of this *cortes*).

it was the custom to call councils for advice. It was also established in this *cortes* that the king could not make a law or change one without consulting the three estates, the clergy, the nobles, the popular or *real*, composed of the *síndicos* or representatives of the *municipios* or *universitats reyals*. Each estate deliberated separately. The clergy usually assisted personally, but the nobles were sometimes represented by jurists. The representatives of the cities were elected by the merchants and industrials and by the guilds.[12] In 1218 representatives from the towns assisted for the first time. In 1299 Don Jaime II established the rule of holding the *cortes* the first Sunday in Lent, alternating at Barcelona and Lérida.

Mallorca and Valencia had three estates. The Aragonese kingdoms had two classes of *cortes*: those called *particulares* (for each state) and those known as *Universidades* (the term used by the jurists of the sixteenth century for corporations) for all the kingdoms in common. These were usually held in a neutral place like Monzón. In the first general *cortes* of 1289 was sanctioned the bond of the Confederation of the Eastern Kingdoms.

The customs and institutions of all were very similar, and the theory behind them identical and the same as the Castilian theory, though in the eastern kingdoms the *cortes* and the *Justicia* which had an organization peculiar to Aragon, operated with more force in checking the tendencies of the monarch to assume the character of a Roman law sovereign, rather than a sovereign of the old Spanish tradition. This was due to a difference of method in fighting against the Moors in the eastern kingdoms and to the hatred of the Aragonese and Catalans for the Roman law.[13]

[12] Ballesteros, III, pp. 496-77.

[13] Fuente, Vicente de la, *Estudios críticos sobre la Historia del derecho de Aragón*, III, p. 335. It was the jurists of the fifteenth century who destroyed the foral law and their principles eventually took possession of the *Justicia.*

All modern historians, Spanish and foreign, recognize the difference and comment upon what they call this constitutional struggle of the Aragonese from the thirteenth century to the advent of the Hapsburgs, namely to limit the royal power and to take from the king the legislative functions which we in modern times have placed in our parliaments. It was a struggle not for such a separate legislative institution, but to keep the sovereign true to the original conception of kingship as the arbiter of justice, the administrator of the kingdom, the expression of authority, with the power to make laws in accordance with the principles of justice and the customs of the land, checked by the advice of the most prudent, learned and important of his subjects, members of his councils and his *cortes*.[14]

The Catalan view of the king's position was the same as that of the Castilians as may be seen from the following:

As through an iniquitous prince without justice and without truth, the land and its inhabitants may be forever destroyed and perish: we the aforementioned princes, Ramón and Adalmodis, of ourselves and with the aid of the noble barons, decree and ordain that all the princes who may succeed us in this principality, should guard always one firm faith, and perfect and true words, in such a manner that all the people, noble and plebians, kings, princes, magnates, *cabelleros*, townsmen and citizens, merchants and traders, travelers and foreigners, friends and enemies, Christians and Saracens, Jews and heretics, may believe in us, and trust to us (that is to our care) not only their person, but also the towns and castles, their honor and estate, their wives

[14] Note the qualifications for membership in the *cortes* of Cataluña. Representatives were to be of "suitable age, great virtue, good discernment and much learning," from the *Cortes* of Montblanch, 1414, quoted in Caroleu e Inglada, Pella y Forgas, *Las Cortes Catalanas*, p. 229.

and children, and whatever they possess in the world without fear and suspicion.[15]

The new monarch had to swear to observe the *Usatges* of Barcelona, the Pacts, treaties and constitutions of the general *cortes*, all customs and usages of the land, in the presence of the *cortes* held in a church in the presence of the clergy to guard against perjury.[16] The king then de iure and de facto, might summon the *cortes* but not before. The king could motu proprio grant privileges and *fueros*, but laws decided on in the *cortes* could not be set aside except with the consent of the *cortes*.[17]

In the thirteenth century, the Aragonese kings had their period of attempting to assume arbitrary powers not conceded to them by the laws and customs. From the reign of Don Alfonso II the Chaste to that of Don Jaime I, the sovereigns remained fairly faithful to the constitutions and *fueros* of their realms reminded no doubt by the motto on the great seal of Aragon, Diligite justitiam qui judicatis terram. During this period, nevertheless, the Roman law theory was consistently being introduced by way of Cataluña, whose contacts with southern France brought her under the influence of the French theorists. These had thought out a brilliant scheme, or a brilliant reconciliation perhaps would be a more just term to describe their ambition, by which the crude customary law of the *fueros* and constitutions could be molded into a polished and flexible body of law in some degree comparable to the brilliant and civilized code of Justinian then so much the object of their studies in the law schools of Toulouse and Montpellier. The idea was to introduce the Justinian principles into those cases not covered by the *Usatges* or local customs. Good sense and

[15] Constitution 65 of the *Usatges*.
[16] *Las Cortes Catalanas*, p. 16.
[17] Ibid., p. 18.

equity were always invoked when tradition was silent and the "written reason" of the Justinian code came easily to the lips of the jurists.

The Justinian principles easily penetrated the written law but it was not so easy to popularize the Roman ideas, to translate them into the popular language and to give them a natural basis in custom. The people did wish a compilation of their laws and *fueros*, and Don Jaime I entrusted this task to the jurist Vidal de Cañellas, a foreigner in a court rather uncultivated and therefore the one most suitable to secure the adoption of the Roman theories. The people were suspicious, even though the king had announced that the codification was not to do more than correct and clarify the old *fueros* and not by any means to add anything contrary to the accepted liberties of the people;[18] popular opposition forced the king to forbid the quoting of the "laws" (*leyes*, that is the written law) as authorities, when the customary laws were sufficient.[19] For the cases not so covered, decision was to be made according to natural reason (*segun la razón natural*). This avoidance of the Roman law turned out to be more apparent than real, since the king's jurists proceeded to interpret the natural reason as the sound reason (*razón sana*) of the Roman equity.

Once the appeal to written reason was made, however, other views than Justinian's could and did appear,—the Roman law anterior to the Justinian compilation, the Theodosian code and the canon law, which was found to be the only rule for many institutions, slavery, wills, property rights, contracts and especially the family.[20] Sufficient con-

---

[18] *Que el suprimir, corregir, ó a clarar ciertos fueros antiguos no habia añadido nada absolutamente á su poder ni restringido en lo más mínimo las acceptables libertades de sus subditos*, Oliver y Esteller, *La Nación y la realeza en los estados de la corona de Aragón*, Madrid, 1884, p. 30.

[19] Oliver y Esteller, *Historia de derecho en Cataluña, Mallorca, Valencia*, I, p. 359.

[20] Oliver y Esteller, Ibid., pp. 352-3, 356.

fusion was introduced by the Roman interpretation of the natural law and reason to bring the situation to a crisis during the reign of Don Jaime. The majority of the people of Aragon selected him for their sovereign in preference to Don Sancho or Don Fernando. It did not take long for Don Jaime to show his ideas. Don Pedro Ahones, a faithful servitor of his father, died and the king proposed to attach his property. This aroused all Aragon against him as it was taken as a revelation of his ideas and his leanings toward the principle of the Roman law, the will of the prince has the force of law. For the first time obedience to the king was denied de facto and civil war threatened.[21] All classes in society without exception joined in a league, the famous *Unión* and finally in the *Cortes* of Tarragona, 1283, brought him to agree to the Privileges of the *Unión.*[22] The first privilege guaranteed the liberty of the subject against the arbitrary rule of the king and placed him under the protection of the *Justicia* of Aragon. The second forbade imprisonment or detention without consent of the *Justicia* in the city of Saragossa and without the consent of the *Cortes* or Aragon or of any other city in the *Unión* of Aragon.[23] Resistance to the crown was legal though extraordinary.[24]

---

[21] The Catalans, more Roman in sympathies than Aragon, favored Don Jaime, and the king tried to get the support of Mallorca but Mallorca, settled in great part by Aragonese, resisted his pretensions and insisted upon the status of an independent state.

[22] *La nación y la realeza en los estados de la corona de Aragón*, p. 26.

[23] For different views on the Privileges, cf. Danvila y Collado, *Las Libertades de Aragón*, Madrid, 1881, pp. 184-255. Zurita, followed by La Fuente, Marichalar y Manrique, holds that the Privileges of the Union was not granted in the *Cortes* of Saragossa in 1287 but were imposed by the nobles and *universidades* of the city. The Privileges do not say that they were granted by the *Cortes*. Such a union had been acknowledged by Don Jaime I. This led to the *Privilegio general* of Don Pedro III and this to the *Privilegio de la Unión* of Don Alfonso III. Marichalar y Manrique claim that the text of this was hidden by Don Pedro IV in order to efface not only the original but the authentic copies or anything having any bearing on it. Zurita found an authorized copy in the archiepiscopal archives of Saragossa, extracts from which he put in his annals. Jerónimo Blancas made a copy later and explained them in his commentaries, but did not dare to print them because of the opposition of Don Philip II. Blancas' book was published in 1878. For texts of the versions of Blancas, Maríchalar y Manrique and the Spanish Academy of History, see *Las Libertades de Aragón*, pp. 234-45.

[24] See the text of the constitution given to Valencia in June, 1340 in *La nación y la realeza*, pp. 78-9. The same recognition was conceded the Catalans, *Hist. del derecho en Cataluña*, I, p. 407.

The struggle was carried on into the reign of Don Pedro III, Don Jaime's successor and imitator. The people rose against him and though Don Pedro prorogued the *Cortes* of Saragossa, he had to agree to the Privileges of the *Unión.* The next two kings, Don Alfonso III and Don Jaime II the Just upheld the *Unión* and the latter granted the Privileges of Tarragona in 1319, from which *cortes* dates the federation of the eastern kingdoms.[25] During the reign of Don Pedro IV a most bitter fight was waged to oppose the Roman policies of the king. He was cruel and tyrannical, Macchiavellian in temperament, and the *Unión* was revived to check his pretensions. This time Cataluña supported Aragon and formed a committee to direct the contest against the king under the leadership of Bernado de Cabrera and Berenguer de Abella. Partly to distract the attention of the people from the issues, within thirty years the king fomented six foreign wars.[26] The *Unión* was under the rule of the *Diputaciones de la generalidad* [27] and finally compelled Don Pedro to yield and summon the *Cortes* of Monzón in 1382,[28] but he prorogued it to the *Cortes* of Saragossa in 1388. In the preamble to this *cortes* the reform of the monarchy was demanded and its jurisdiction defined.[29]

A reform project was drawn up by the Archbishop of Saragossa, one of the ablest students of political theory of the times, and presented on behalf of the ecclesiastical and popular estates.[30] The ideas of the preamble repeat those of the medieval tradition: Sovereignty and authority is from God and the king must rule in justice and be solicitous for

[25] Quicumque sit rex Aragonum inde etiam sit rex regni Valentiae et comes Barchinonae, Aureum opus, quoted in *La nación y la realeza,* p. 83, note 102.
[26] *La nación y la realeza,* p. 45.
[27] The *Diputación generalidad,* modeled on the *Diputación* of Aragon, appeared in the latter part of the fourteenth century. It had the function of publishing and explaining the acts of the *cortes* and the *fueros,* dealt with infractions of these, and passed upon all disputes between the people and the king in respect to his authority.
[28] For text of this see *La nación y la realeza,* Appendix III, pp. 93 sq.
[29] For the preamble see Ibid., Appendix, IV, p. 97 sq.
[30] For text of the project, Ibid., Appendix V, p. 101 sq.

the welfare of the people.[31] The project contains sixty-seven titles and suggests the reorganization of the supreme council, the members to be named by the king in consultation with the *cortes.* These were not to be removed without just cause subject to investigation by a committee of the *cortes.* All royal orders were to receive the approval of the chancellor and a majority of the members of the council. All royal officials exercising jurisdiction in each kingdom were to be irremovable during their term of office, usually three years, unless by agreement of the chancellor and a majority of the counselors, with a *residencia.*[32] These suggestions hint at the methods by which the king had been assuming absolutist powers. By appointing those trained in the Roman theories and removing them arbitrarily, should any of them oppose him, the king had been gradually departing from the traditional spirit and organs of government.

Oliver y Esteller considers this project to be the germ of the government of the nation by the nation, but this is reading modern terms into the past. A study of the preamble and titles in detail clearly show that it was but a return to the medieval tradition. The project was not adopted owing to divisions among the nobles fomented and exploited by palace intrigues. A counter project was proposed by the Count of Urgel, a member of the royal family on behalf of the nobles, much more in line with the Roman law theories. This precipitated a debate over the election of the counselors in which the regalist party was losing when the king resorted to stirring up a distraction on the French frontier to break up the sessions of the *cortes* (December 28,

---

[31] *La seyoria e potestat mundanal es per nostre Senyor Deus donada e comanada als Reys los quals ab continua sollicitud profunda saviesa e immutabile justicia han a regir los Reynes e pobles segons de la sollicitud dehia Casiodorus en ses Epistolis que aquel qui te lo subiran stament en la cosa publica deu esser sollicit a totes coses car no pot haver sanitat en lo cors si donchs no la han los membres. . . .*

[32] *La nación y la realeza,* pp. 56-58.

1389). The argument over this gave an opportunity to the Queen to take a hand and to have introduced a third project allowing the king greater prerogatives in choosing the counselors.[33] The invasion of Cataluña gave the king the chance to prorogue the *cortes.*

The dissensions in the *cortes* thus begun only paved the way for the king to rule through various intrigues. The counselors received ironical titles from the people, such as dominus mundi, Deus in terris, dominus omnium, lex animata in terris, etc., but sarcasm was no weapon with which to defeat the ambitions of the Roman lawyers. It was by such quarrels and the consequent befogging of the issues, that the fight for Aragonese liberties was lost long before Don Philip II delivered the *coup de grace.* That Don Philip could not do this without a most bitter struggle, was due to the hold the popular tradition had upon the minds and imaginations of the people, and to the office of the *Justicia.*

The *Justicia* or *Justicia mayor* was a special magistrate, unique in Spain, to act as arbiter between the *cortes* and the nation and the nation and the king and to defend the guarantees of the rights of the people. Research has not yet agreed on the origins of this institution. Balaguer holds to the tradition that it was contemporaneous with the Aragonese monarchy. La Fuente considers the *Justicia* to have originated very modestly as an official, learned in the law, and selected by the king to do justice for him if the king were too busy with war to do it himself—*una especie de auditor de guerra.* Aragon was but an armed camp until the time of Don Alfonso *el Batallador.* From 1000 to 1140 the *Justicia* was more a *vicario* or delegate, which remained his status until the thirteenth century.[34] In this century he took over the fight

[33] For text of this see the *Cortes* of June 23, 1389.
[34] De la Fuente, V., *Estudios críticos sobre la hist. de del derecho de Aragón.*

against the Roman law. Don Jaime II increased his power and appointed some worthy men to the office. The decision of the *Justicia* was final; he was sole judge of delinquent officials and passed upon all interpretations of the law. His permanent seat was at Saragossa. From 1441 he could not be removed without the consent of the *cortes.* In 1461 his assistant lieutenants were chosen by lot and served for one year. They were empowered to call together the legal authorities of the kingdom and the dicta of this concilium extraordinarium were preserved and regarded as regular laws. By 1390 the *cortes* had appointed a committee of four, representative of the four estates, to receive complaints against the *Justicia.* Later the number was raised to seventeen and care taken not to have them all lawyers. The *Justicia* had wide powers. The chief functions may be reduced to two: to watch over the infringement of the laws of the land, and to protect the rights of each against the tyranny of all. By the *manifestación* the *Justicia* protected prisoners, especially those awaiting judgments, from all ill-treatment. The *manifestación* protected the property of the accused from those who might be anxious to seize it, by depositing it under the charge of some one person who would give security and produce it (*manifestaría*) when it was asked of him.[35] There was a special prison for these, the *carcel de los manifestados.* The term *manifestación* does not appear until the fourteenth century. From the tenth to the thirteenth century the king granted this relief, but in the second half of the following century, the *Justicia* took charge of it. It was found also in Cataluña with the name of *caplieuta* (caput levare). By the *firmas,* special guarantees were given to those who feared

[35] Ballesteros, III, p. 489.

judgments contrary to the laws; a *firma* suspended trial until the *Justicia* had time to look into the case.[36]

The part the *cortes* was expected to play as an institution of government was to provide advice and consultation for the king. In the *Cortes* of León, 1188, Don Alfonso IX promised to the prelates and magnates assembled cum electis civibus ex singulis civitatibus, not to make war or peace or treaties without the consent of the bishops, nobles and good men, "through whose advice I ought to be guided." [37] Colmeiro gives this as the first mention of the power of the *cortes,* though the king only bound himself to ask advice, not to take it. He reserved the right to use his own judgment. The king simply bound himself to do what was expected of him by custom and the maxims of the Forum Iudiciorum. As the embodiment of authority, representing justice and not the people, he was of course expected to take the responsibility of decision and the *cortes* was the logical agency developed to offer advice, though not the only one.

In the prologue [38] to the *Cortes* of Toledo, 1480, this is brought out clearly. "They should love justice who judge the land, and judgment very severe will be passed against those who govern the land. For this the Catholic Kings were constantly on the look-out for justice, and since justice makes one straight before God, Who is a just Judge and the highest Judge, there must be a rule for this, and the rule is the law which is the guardian of that which makes straight the

---

[36] Ballesteros, P., *Origen de la firma de derecho ante el Justicia de Aragón,* Madrid, 1904.

[37] Promisi etiam quod non faciam guerram, vel pacem vel placitum nisi cum concilio episcoporum nobilium et bonorum per quorum consilium debo regi, *Actas de las Córtes de León y Castilla,* I, p. 40.

There is a dispute over the meaning of the term placitum. Colmeiro holds here that it means treaty, since in the traditional conception of sovereignty, the king had the legislative power, but du Cange does not admit this interpretation. He considers placitum to mean iussum et voluntas. For discussion of this, see Torréanaz, pp. 121-2, note 1. Colmeiro has the weight of tradition and the codes on his side.

[38] *Actas de las Cortes de los antiguos reinos de León y Castilla,* IV, p. 110.

life and acts of men before God. Since so much depends upon the law, it is meet that the one who makes it, should act with great deliberation as to what is necessary. Hence we have called our *Cortes* so as to discuss and oversee the things which may be necessary for the good government of these kingdoms, and we shall present various petitions, and the *Cortes* shall supplicate us, on such things we may order to promote and remedy according as agrees with the service of God, or ourselves, and the good of the commonweal (*bien de la republica*), and pacify the estates of our kingdom, and when this is done in accordance with the prelates, *cabelleros* and doctors of our councils, we proceed to ordain the laws which follow. . . ."

The Catalan *cortes* had the custom of presenting to the king a memorial of grievances (*greuges*) in the judicial or political order.[39] The king responded and adjudicated affairs, thus the *cortes* formed a kind of high tribunal where could be received the greatest guarantees of justice. Often the king nominated a committee of jurists who jointly with the *provisores de greuges* chosen by the *cortes*, deliberated on the question. These had to hand down a decision within ten months after the matter was submitted to them and excommunication was the penalty for a decision not in accordance with justice and equity, or the *Usatges* or constitutions, acts of the *cortes* and customs of the land.[40] During the fourteenth and up to the middle of the sixteenth century, the *Procesos de Gravamenes* dealt almost exclusively with conflicts under the civil law and of jurisdiction, very little on high policies of state.

The Castilian *cortes* had the right of petitioning the crown from 1293 and the exercise of the right became a regular

[39] This dates from the constitution *Ordenam e statuim que si mal feyt* of Don Alfonso II in the *Cortes* of Monzon, and also under Don Jaime II and Don Pedro III.

[40] *Las Cortes Catalanas*, p. 118.

practice after 1317. The subject matter of such petitions might cover all the departments of government where abuses were considered to exist. In these functions of petition, many writers have seen the germ of what they call the "right of legislation." The following quotation is typical of this view: "That the Castilian assembly was unable to turn this right of petition into a right of legislation (as did the English Parliament in this period) was due to its ineffectual procedure, to its failure to make redress precede supply, and to the general lack of coöperation and to the political opportunism which characterized the members." [41]

The Castilian *cortes* did not claim the right of legislation because it was not in its tradition to expect this. The whole theory upon which the Spanish *cortes* or whichever kingdom, was based, precluded this. It was always the manifestation of that Spanish concept of society as made up of a series of related interests, the regulation of which with a view to the general welfare devolved upon the king. As the different classes slowly developed in society it was natural that they should find representation in that body which would voice their interests and advise the king in respect to these. The institution itself was based upon a theory of representation and at no time upon the notion of individual wills. It was not the expression of mass intelligence. It had nothing in it of the Rousseauistic theory of representation. It was in short the legitimate representation of the ideas and aspirations of all those classes—or *socios* as one author puts it—which were interested in the duration and progress of political society. Hence no one was called to sit in the *cortes* who was not a person or a corporation truly interested in social prosperity. Such juridical entities properly constituted the state. These are the entities which support the individual and through them he finds his opportunity

[41] Merrimam, R. B., Rise of the Spanish Empire, New York, 1918, I, p. 227.

for development and protection. They sum up the three great institutions of all civilizations, the family, religion, property, and hence the representation was crystallized in the three estates, ecclesiastical, military, popular.

"And as in these groupings so philosophically ordered, the individual did not figure save as the representative of a social interest, the prelates assisted at the *cortes* in the name of the diocese, the abbots as delegates from their convents, the barons by reason of their seignorial interests, and by the law governing each in their respective spheres, they lost their representation on that day on which they failed to show the character in virtue of which they had acquired it." [42]

The concession of the *servicio* by the *cortes* of Castile and León was in line with this thought. The origin of this is lost in the shadow of the Middle Ages.[43] It seems to follow from the admitting of the *procuradores* to the *cortes.* Though the Kings of Castile could not tax arbitrarily, it was not necessary for them to have the consent of the *cortes.* The *Cortes* of Madrid, 1391, arranging details for the tutors of Don Enrique III, said these (the tutors) could tax without the consent of the *Cortes.* The king could not levy new taxes, demand extraordinary grants, or new coins, or the *alcabala* without summoning the *cortes.* The legal coins (*moneda forera*) and the ordinary taxes, such as the *fonsadera, yantares, marzadga* or *martiniega* were obligatory according to the *fueros.* All taxes originated in custom and not by legislative act. Loans were not necessarily at the will of the *cortes* though some *cortes* insisted on the consent of the *procuradores* (Madrid, 1391, 1393). At times the *cortes* would budget the expenses of the royal household and ask account of the expenditures of extraordinary loans. A com-

[42] *Las Cortes Catalanas,* pp. 71-2.

[43] Colmeiro, Introduction to *Actas de las Cortes de los reinos de Castilla y León,* I, p. 72.

mon financial operation was the alteration of the values of the coinage (called by the Portuguese *quebrar moeda*) and against this the *cortes* protested repeatedly. Petitions of the *cortes* granted by the sovereign had obligatory force. In the *Cortes* of Briviesca (1387) it was decided that laws and enactments already in force could not be modified without consultation with the *cortes*, though the king reserved his right of making new laws according to custom. The *cortes* received the oath of the new sovereign to respect the laws, customs and *fueros* and the *cortes* swore allegiance to the heir to the throne. In general the *cortes* was the voice of popular sentiment, and with its right of petition had considerable influence on the administration of the government as a deliberative and consultative body.[44] The principle involved was not the power of the people but the effect on social interests.

The importance of this is seen when one examines the membership of the *cortes*. It was not necessary as in the Eastern kingdoms, for all three estates to attend each *cortes*. But a *cortes* would be considered illegal in which taxes were discussed unless those who were to pay them were represented, as this naturally touched a very important interest. Likewise, the discussion on war or peace, required the presence of the nobility who with their force would be directly concerned in such a matter.[45]

This explains many things in the procedure of the *cortes* which modern critics find awkward or inept. To take a few examples at random: The plural voting in the Catalan *cortes*, whereby the extra votes were assigned according to importance, the greater number going to the Primate Archbishop.[46] (Vota non sunt numeranda sed ponderanda). The

[44] Ballesteros, III, pp. 338-9.
[45] Ballesteros, III, p. 540.
[46] Cf. Constitution: Votem statuim of Don Pedro the Great, reflecting the Digest, Quod pars curiae. . . .

voting was not based upon arithmetic, as so many modern attempts to imitate it suppose, but upon relative importance of the social interests. It was also aimed to secure better distributive justice in the social order and to prevent tyrannies of either the majority or the minority.[47]

When the corporative interests of the *municipio*, cities, and towns came to be included in the *cortes*, it was necessary for some system of election to be adopted, as it was obviously impossible for them to attend in person. Once this was introduced the way was opened for the clash of personal interests and personal ambitions, and to guard against these evils and the resulting complications, ingenious and elaborate precautions were taken. This is why voting by lot was so popular. It avoided bargains ahead of time and such party dissensions as were bound to grow up under another system. Its advantages were always considered to outweigh its disadvantages.

In early times the *Veguer* of Barcelona was accustomed to summon the heads of families (*caps de casa*) to the public plaza where by a majority vote of all present, the *síndicos* or deputies to the *cortes* were chosen. The hour of meeting was either the fall of the evening, when the men would be returning from their work, or at sunrise when they would be starting out. In 1387 a new system of indirect election was adopted. The *concejo de ciento* (council of one hundred), elected a committee of twelve (four merchants, two artisans, two tradespeople, four citizens) to draw up by order a list of candidates from which by majority secret vote the *síndicos* were to be selected. By a similar method a *junta* of twenty-four proportionately from each class, formed a consulting committee, permanent in each city, to advise the *síndicos*. It was called the *Vintiguatrena de Cort.* Voting by lot was introduced by Don Ferdinand the Catholic in

[47] *Las Cortes Catalanas*, p. 117.

1493. This commission was intended to secure the direct will of the people at all times and to prevent the *síndicos* becoming representative of a party.[48]

For the same reason the *Universidades* of Cataluña would revoke the credentials of the *síndicos* if they exceeded their instructions in the *cortes.*[49] Various committees of arbitration were arranged to settle all disputes among the various estates, so as to arrive at a solution and prevent dissensions. Each estate had its lawyers and its spokesmen to deliver its mind to the other orders. The ecclesiastical estate kept the official copies of all the acts of the *cortes* and in general every precaution was taken to the end that disputes be minimized, interests reconciled and dissensions concluded. Within six months the notary of the *cortes* had to deliver to the deputies authentic copies of all the proceedings.[50]

Similar precautions were taken in the Castilian *cortes* for similar reasons though not so carefully guarded as in the eastern kingdoms. There was no rule for the number of representatives for each class. That varied at the will of the monarch until the reign of the Catholic Kings. Some towns always sent representatives, others did not but all could be called. Seventeen were regularly summoned, later the number was raised to twenty-two. Don Alfonso IX issued a general call to the cities of his kingdom, which chose the citizens or citizens which had represented them in the *Cortes* of León in 1188. At the *Cortes* of *Carrión* in the same year, assisted the *majores* of forty-eight cities and towns. No name of any *procurador* has been preserved in the proceedings of the twelfth century.[51]

---

[48] *Las Cortes Catalanas*, pp. 77-80.

[49] *Cortes* of Montblanch, 1307. For an interesting account of a sixteenth century example, see *Las Cortes Catalanas*, pp. 88-94, for the *Cortes general* of Monzón in 1585 under Don Philip II.

[50] *Córtes* of Alcañis and Saragossa, 1441.

[51] Ballesteros, II, p. 512.

According to Gama Barros, the *procuradores* in general were chosen from the highest class in the *municipios*, which was the *omes bonos.* In the charter of the *Hermandad* of the *concejos* of Castile in 1295, it is said: "*Quando los conceyos de la hermandat habieren de enviar omes bonos de su conceyo quier a la Corts . . . que los envirén de los meyores del logar.*" (When the *concejos* of the *Hermandad* have to send good men of their *concejo* to the *cortes* let them send the best men of the place.) Already by the fifteenth century, the attempt of the crown may be seen to suggest certain men as *procuradores.* The *Cortes* of Burgos complained of this as did other *cortes* of the same century.[52] That not all were summoned regularly was due to the failure of some *concejos* to send their representatives, perhaps because of the expense.[53] The custom of sending representatives began to die out then and such towns as continued to send representatives began to stress the idea of privilege being attached to their vote and to wish to keep the representation small.[54] This change was the result of Roman law ideals and a departure from the ancient custom. All during the thirteenth century the representatives were summoned to represent the inhabitants of each town.[55] They were the true voice of the towns, carried definite instructions and could not depart from these. As Colmeiro says, it was really the *Concejo* which was represented by a legal faction.[56]

Consequently there is nothing more clear than that the Spanish idea of representation was one not of class interest but of social interests. This sociological concept, as moderns would put it, derives from the old Augustinian theory of

---

[52] Ballesteros, III, pp. 332-4.

[53] Ibid.

[54] Introduction to *Actas de las Cortes,* I, p. 27. The *Cortes* of Ocana, 1469, pet. 6; *Cortes* of Burgos, 1512, pet. 10. Don Felipe and Doña Juana in the *Cortes* of Valladolid in 1506 and Don Ferdinand the Catholic in the *Cortes* of Burgos in 1512 refused.

[55] The *Cortes* of León, 1188, called them citizens (cives). The use of the term *procurador del concejo* began in the *Cortes* of Medino del Campo, 1305 and was fixed in the *Cortes* held there in 1313. The clergy had used this term in the *Cortes* of Valladolid in 1295, *Actas de las Cortes,* p. 28.

[56] Ibid., p. 37.

civil society. It recognizes the essential interests and bases of society and strove to hold true the balance among them. In a society where all recognized the government to have the aim of securing justice, so that each individual could realize his ends here in order to attain his final end hereafter, there could be no real conflict of interests and hence no reason to compromise them.

That idea of conflicting class interests came in with the Roman law and ended by stultifying the institutions developed and in inflicting a blight upon Spain from which she still suffers.

Owing to the more aristocratic type of society which the fortunes of the wars of the Reconquest developed in Castile the Roman law there earlier is seen to have gained a foothold and on the ruin of the Castilian *cortes* followed the ruin of those of the Aragonese kingdoms.

Up to the fifteenth century the *concejos* had freely chosen their representatives to the *cortes* but during the disordered reigns of Don Juan II and Don Enrique IV, the municipalities began to become corrupt. The authority of the *alcaldes* and *regidores* was weakened by venialty and the Crown interfered in the elections in consequence of the Roman law interpretation of the sovereign's position and authority. The kings were desirous of playing the towns off against the nobles. The Catholic Kings endeavored to reform these conditions by introducing voting by lot. With Don Philip and Doña Juana and Don Charles V, the struggle to secure control of the representatives of the towns was renewed, so that the Flemish party could secure candidates favorable to their cause in the *Cortes*.[57] The preceding century had prepared the way for representation on personal interests rather than social, and though the transition was bitterly fought the *Communidades* lost.

[57] Sandoval, *Hist. Emp. Carlos V*, Lib. III, IV.

In the call to the *Cortes* of Santiago and Coruña in 1520, Don Charles V laid down the stipulation that the representatives should bring to the *cortes* ample powers to discuss whatever might come up, and this obliged the *concejos* to break with the ancient tradition of sending their *procuradores* with strictly limited and definite powers. Cristóbal Pinelo, from Seville, ironically inquired whether they were to serve as slaves to the lord.[58] Many of the towns yielded, already accustomed to following the king's will, but there were many protests during the reigns of Don Charles V and Don Philip II. The king took various measures to dominate the *concejos*, requiring the *procuradores* to submit to the President of the *cortes* their instructions and ordered the *corregidores* to negotiate with the *concejos* on all disputes and to send to the king the votes of the *regidores* signed by the secretary of the *concejo*. Don Philip II was more suave but the final act was accomplished during his reign.

In 1515 at the *Cortes* of Burgos, Don Ferdinand inaugurated the novelty of asking the representatives to keep secret the subject matter of discussion, which was decidedly against custom as Juan de Fonseca, Bishop of Burgos, reminded him, and in the *Cortes* of Madrid, 1563, an oath was taken to keep all matters secret save by permission of the king.[59] The *procuradores* were not obliged to give an account of their acts to the *concejo*, but usually did so and in the *Cortes* of Santiago and Coruña of 1520 the king was petitioned to require them to return to the *Concejo* and to give an account within forty days after the session on pain of losing their salary and office.

By 1570 the rich had gained control of the *concejos* and hence the representatives were working against the interests of their estates. A petition of the *Cortes* of that year com-

[58] Introduction to *Actas de las Córtes,* p. 40.
[59] Sandoval, Lib. VIII, par. i.

plained that the towns were governed by the rich and asked that only nobles be chosen for the position of sheriffs and members of the *concejos.* This was of course against the interests of the burgesses, who held the preponderance in the *concejo.* Perhaps it was wise to have the sheriffs selected from among the wealthy to put them beyond temptation, since few of the nobles were rich as a result of the effects of the law of primogeniture.[60] Placing the representation in the control of the rich, however, tended to keep the issues narrowly confined to the interests of wealth and contributed in no small part to the destruction of true democratic government.

[60] Sempère y Guarino, *Histoire des Cortès d'Espagne*, Bordeaux, 1815, p. 215.

FERDINAND AND ISABELLA

Chapter IX

Conclusion

THE Spanish theory of government revolved around two poles of thought: One—the principles of society were the social interests which drew men together in a common fellowship and a common solidarity, not alone because of their economic and material needs, but more particularly and essentially because of their possession of a common origin and a common destiny. The society was unified because mankind was unified in the one Faith. To the ius gentium of the Roman empire which drew men together because of the material needs, there succeeded the internationalism of the Church, which drew men together by the force of a superior principle, which while recognizing the material interests went beyond them and subordinated them to man's higher interests. Society was based upon the Christianitas of the individual which gave rise to Christendom in which there was but the one citizenship as in Rome, based not upon submission to a common power as in Rome but upon the one baptism. These social interests affecting as they do all the relationships which men inevitably establish as they come into contact with each other, could but lead to conflict or result in an *impasse*, unless there were some directing authority which would resolve the conflicts into that peace and harmony which St. Augustine called pax.

How was this to be done? In the answer the Spanish developed their second principle. Each interest must have its due but the due was not recognized as unconditioned. It was to be determined in relation to the ends served, which in turn were relative to the final end of man. Justice then was seen to be a matter of conditions and relations. As St. Augustine observed:[1] "Peace between man and God is the well ordered concord. Domestic peace is the well ordered concord between those of the family who rule and those who obey. Civil peace is a similar concord among the citizens. The peace of the celestial city is the perfectly ordered and harmonious enjoyment of God, and of one another in God. The peace of all things is the tranquillity of order. Order is the distribution which allots things equal and unequal, each to its own place." "Since this earthly peace is to bear upon the peace of Heaven,"[2] justice must be more than a practical order of material interests. It must be based upon order as determined by the Eternal Law, and the laws embodying it must transcend mere rules intended to regulate interests, since their primary purpose should be to supply principles of human actions and thus to regulate conduct.

Government must then be a directing agency, a *regiment*, and the one invested with authority, should stand aloof, partaking of none of the particular interests which he has to direct, but serving all. The Spanish believed that the monarchy could assume this function and therefore the king was to be the servus servorum and not the dominus omnium.[3] His charge was to exercise the authority in obedience to God, in charity and justice. As God was the source of all law and of all authority, it was in the study of God that he would find the wisdom to administer the necessary justice in his

[1] De Civitate Dei, xix, c. 13.
[2] Ibid. c. 17.
[3] See the advice of the dying Philip II to his son: . . . un principe como vos se ha de servir de todos y de cada uno en su oficio, sin sujetaros a nadie, ni dejaros gobernar conocidamente de ningumo sine oid a mucho y reservar el secreto necessario a cada uno, para elección de lo meyor con libertad como dueno y cabeza de todas. Cil. Gonzales Davila, *Hist. de Felipe III, Lib.* I, *c.* xii.

kingdom. Consequently the direction of his actions must flow from conscience, to the observance of the moral order and thence to the regulation of the material interests of society. His justice becomes the application of the Divine justice to the problem of ruling his subjects, regulating, arranging and disposing of them under its sanctions. And in doing this he tends to perfect society, that union of hearts, wills and concord, the pactum societatis.

In the Spanish conception of government, the king had the double function of the ruler and the institutional symbol. As an institution his function extended to the whole field of government, executive, deliberative (deliberative rather than legislative, since law as something made originated from custom and not the will of the sovereign), and judicial. The checks on the possible abuse of such powers in the hands of one, were first sought through the king's conscience, second through the consultation with the subjects either by way of the *cortes* or the councils, thirdly holding the king to be subject to the principle of the supremacy of law as determined by the terms of the coronation oath.

The *cortes* and council took on more properly the deliberative function, for in them were to be found the experienced statesmen, whose prudent advice and considered decisions had great influence with the sovereign. The councils "were all the knowledge, power and understanding of the prince, his eyes, his hands, his feet, the motive of his heroic actions,"[4] the keystone of his machinery of ruling.

The various interests of society, the aristocratic, the religious, the popular, the city, town or rural district, the corporation, guild and league (*hermandad*) were all framed in the *fueros* applying to each class, and the *cortes* was

[4] Sánchez de Toca, J., *Del Gobierno en el Regimen Antiguo y en el Parlementario,* Madrid, 1890, pp. 71, 72, 169.

developed to provide the equilibrium of these class interests. Thus upholding their *fueros* as guarantees of their rights, these interests acted as a powerful check on any usurpation of the royal power. At the same time also they took their share in the deliberative function of government, though not to the same extent as the councils, since being representative they were not sufficiently detached to be impartial.[5]

The sovereign remained as always the juridical representative of the supreme civil authority, and as such the essential principle of the life and unified action of civil society. In himself, by reason of its royal dignity, or its essence as the Scholastics would say, he had to bear always the direct personal action of ruling. In him were harmonized the general interests of society. The law making him king did not endow him with the understanding and character to win the spontaneous veneration of his subjects. The king should be the born statesman. As Fadrique Furio remarked to Don Philip II, "There are three ways of understanding; one understanding comprehends and knows by its own efforts, the other is advised and instructed, the other is neither. This last is useless and born to be in perpetual slavery; the second is good, but the first is divine and entitled by right to command and govern. The efficacy of the second depends on its discernment or power to separate the good from the evil . . . ; but the good prince is the one who can take counsel with himself and availing himself of

---

[5] As the interests in the *cortes* became representative of personal forces and ambitions, instead of the necessary classes in society, they lost their reason for being, and hence the people saw with indifference, the elimination of the two estates in 1538. Sánchez de Toca thinks that since the *cortes* changed into representatives of oligarchies rather than interests, the Catholic Kings were moved to the reform of the councils, so as to create a new body to oppose the pretensions of the oligarchies,—that is, the nobles became a territorial oligarchy instead of an aristrocracy, and the municipal corporations became the oligarchy of the bourgeoisie (Ibid. p. 63).

the counsel of others, as well as of his own and others, he may direct to what is demanded by the nature of the business, persons, according to place and time, and thus lead gloriously to the end." [6]

With this conception of government in mind, it is easy to grasp how insidiously dangerous were the theories introduced by the Roman jurists. The surface likeness between the two concepts was striking but the setting was vastly different. The Spanish and the Spanish society were set in a framework of justice, the justice of the City of God. The Roman prince and the Roman empire were set in the framework of will, the more arbitrary and absolute in that it was theoretically held to be the will of the people. "For the Romans from early times it was the power of the will that animated the whole body of the law." [7] The only check on will was to be found in more will. "They considered that they had a liberty all the greater, the greater the firmness and constancy of the individual which arrested the abuses of power. Liberty was a check on liberty. . . . All law moreover was held to proceed from the people and to derive its restraining force from them. . . . It followed that as the power of the people was absolute, those who possessed imperium were held to be endowed with powers equal to those of the people whose delegates they were. . . . They had the same sovereignty and exercised it in an absolute manner, for this was the very meaning of the term imperium. The praetor in declaring the law legislated out of the plenitude of his own will in his exercise of the legislative power of the people." [8] The will of the prince had the force of law.

[6] Prologue to his *El Concejo y consejeros del principe;* also Sánchez de Toca, Ibid., pp. 258-60.
[7] Sound Democratic Principles in Catholic Tradition, Rev. Moorhouse I. X. Millar, S.J., in "Thought" for March, 1928.
[8] Ibid.

The ultimate base of the Roman principle being then the naked force of the will, Roman society eventually fell asunder as a result of its unrestrained and undirected will to power. There was no point upon which opposition, either philosophical or physical, could develop to retain its frenzy or modify its excesses. The general interests of society succumbed to the excesses of individualism.

Such a principle introduced into the Spanish formulas of society and its theory, came to grips with a living principle which was the expression of reality. It could not therefore destroy Spanish society as it destroyed Rome, but it paralyzed Spanish energies and confused their sense of direction and warped out of all proportion to the traditional lines of its development, the beautiful Spanish scheme which antecedently had been in process of construction.

Creative thought was nipped in the bud, just as the scene was set for the most trying and severe test of its strength, the civilizing of the lands discovered by Columbus. The impossible attempt which the Spanish jurists were making to translate their legal philosophy and political institutions into the mold of Stoic thought, handicapped their plan of governing these territories politically. Socially and ethically the Spanish philosophy remained free from the Stoic influence, and hence in meeting and mastering the primitive temperament and alien culture of the Indians, the Spaniards found greater success. This explains the humanitarian features of the Code of the Indies so much admired by its critics. But the real lessons to be learned from all this, is not a philosophy of humanitarianism, but the necessity, if good government is to be attained, of harmonizing both the social and the political philosophies into a synthesis based upon an adequate concept of Justice. For this an understanding of, and a return to, the philosophy of St. Augustine in so far as it has been supplemented by St. Thomas and the later Scholastics is imperative.[9]

[9] For an interesting note on the contrast between the Stoic and the Augustinian concept of Justice, consult Rev. Moorhouse I. X. Millar, S.J., in "Thought" for September, 1929.

SPANISH MEDIEVAL TOWN AND WARFARE

BIBLIOGRAPHY

BIBLIOGRAPHIES:

BALLESTER Y CASTELL, R.:

Las Fuentes narrativas de la Historia de España, Palma de Mallorca, 1908.

SANCHEZ, ALONZO:

Fuentes de la Historia Española e Hispano-americana, Madrid, 1927.

PRIMARY SOURCES:

DOCUMENTS AND CODES:

Los Códigos Españoles, 2 vols., Madrid, 1847-57.

Collección de doc. inéditos para la Historia de España, Madrid, 1842-95.

Collección de doc. inéditos relativos al desc. conquista y org. de las antiguas pos. españoles de ultra mar, 2nd series, Madrid, 1890-7.

Córtes de los antiguos reinos de Aragón y de Valencia y Principado de Cataluña, pub. by the Royal Academy of History, Madrid, 1896.

Córtes de los antiguos reinos de León y de Castilla, Madrid, 1883-4.

Código de las Costumbres de Tortosa, Madrid, 1881, vol. IV of Oliver y Esteller, *Historia del derecho Cataluña.*

Doc. para la Historia de las Instituciones de León y Castilla (Siglos X-XIII), Madrid, 1919.

Recopilación de las Leyes de las Indías, Madrid, 1774, 3rd ed.

MIGNE:

Patres Latini, Vols. 81-84, for texts of the Councils of Toledo and the works of Isidore of Seville.

OROSIUS:

Adversum paganos historiarum libri vii, in *Corp. Lat. Script.* Vienna, 1882.

BIBLIOGRAPHY

SECONDARY SOURCES:

Altamira y Crevea, *Historia de España*, Barcelona, 1919.

Balaguer, *Historia de Cataluña y de la Corona de Aragón*, Barcelona, 1860-3.

Ballesteros y Beretta, A., *Historia de España y su Influencia en la Historia Universal*, Barcelona, 1918-26.

La Fuente, M. de, *Historia general de España*, Madrid, 1889.

Mariana, *Historia general de España*, Madrid, 1608.

Sandoval, *Historia de la vida de Carlos V*, Pamplona, 1614.

MISCELLANEOUS:

ANTEQUERA:

Historia de la legislación española, Madrid, 1874.

BALAGUER, V.:

Instituciones y reyes de Aragón, Saragossa, 1896.

BECKER, J.:

La Política española en las Indías, Madrid, 1920.

La tradición política española, Madrid, 1896.

CAÑAL, CARLOS:

San Isidoro, Seville, 1897.

CÁNOVAS DEL CASTILLO:

Historia de la Decadencia de España, Madrid, 1910, 2nd ed.

CAROLEU Y INGLADA, PELLA Y FORGAS:

Las Córtes Catalanas, 2nd ed. Barcelona, 1876.

CEDILLO, CONDE DE:

El Cardenal Cisneros, Madrid, 1921.

COLMEIRO:

Derecho Administrativo, Madrid, 1876.

El Poder civil, Madrid, 1884-6.

COMBÈS:

La Doctrine politique de St. Augustin, Paris, 1927.

DANVILA Y COLLADO:

El Poder civil, Madrid, 1885-6, (bibliography).

Las Libertades de Aragón, Madrid, 1881.

LA FUENTE, V. DE:

Estudios críticos, sobre la Historia y el derecho de Aragón, 3 vols. Madrid, 1884-6.

HAUSER:

La Nouvelle orientation économique, Paris, 1924.

BIBLIOGRAPHY

HINOJOSA, E. DE:

El Elemento germánico en el derecho español, Madrid, 1915.

Influencia que tuvieron en el derecho publico de su patria y singularamente en el derecho penal los filósofos y teólogos, Madrid, 1890.

Estudios sobre la Historia del derecho español, Madrid, 1903.

L'AIGLESIA, F. DE:

Estudios de criticos históricos, Madrid, 1919.

MARIÉJOL:

L'Espagne sous Ferdinande et Isabelle, Paris, 1892.

MARTÍNEZ-MARINA, F.:

Ensayo histórico crítico sobre la Antigua legislación, Madrid, 1808.

Teoría de las Córtes, Madrid, 1820.

MERRIMAN, R. B.:

Rise of the Spanish Empire in the Old World and the New, New York, 3 vols., 1918-25.

MILLAR, MOORHOUSE I. X., S.J.:

Origin of Sound Democratic Principles in Catholic Tradition in *Thought*, New York, March, 1928; *St. Augustine and Cicero's Definition of the State* in *Thought*, September, 1929.

MUÑOZ Y ROMERO:

Col. de Fueros municipales, Madrid, 1847.

OLIVER Y ESTELLER:

Historia del derecho en Cataluña y Mallorca, Madrid, 1881, 4 vols.

PÉREZ-PUJOL, E.:

Historia de las Instituciones sociales de la España-Goda, Madrid, 1896, 4 vols.

PIDAL:

Lecciones sobre la Historia del gobierno y legislación de España, Madrid, 1880.

SACRISTAN Y MARTÍNEZ:

Municipalidades de Castilla y León, Madrid, 1877.

SÁNCHEZ Y TOCA, J.:

Gobierno en el régimen antiguo y el Parlementario, Madrid, 1890.

SERRANO Y SANZ:

Origines de la dominación española en América, Madrid, 1918.

BIBLIOGRAPHY

SEMPÈRE Y GUARINO:
Histoire de Cortès d'Espagne Bordeaux, 1815.

SIMONET, ED.:
El Concilio III Toledo, Madrid, 1891.

ST. THOMAS:
De Legibus, 2:1, Quaest. 90-114.
De Regimine principum, Turin, 1924.

TORRÉANAZ, CONDE DE:
Los consejos del Rey durante la Edad Media, Madrid, 1884.

UREÑA Y SMENJAUD, R. DE:
La Legislación Gótico-Hispano, Madrid, 1905.

ZYBURA, ED.:
Present Day Thinkers and the New Scholasticism, St. Louis, 1926.

INDEX

INDEX

INDEX

INDEX

www.ingramcontent.com/pod-product-compliance
Lightning Source LLC
LaVergne TN
LVHW091530200926
848483LV00002B/351